God Still Protects

Does (54) Amazing Testimonies of Gods Divine Protection

Dr Michael H Yeager

ISBN-10:1533116776
ISBN-13:9781533116772

DEDICATION

We dedicate this book to those who are truly hungry and thirsty to live in the realm of the super natural, and to those who have already tasted of the heavenly realm. We dedicate this to the bride of Christ, those who are called to go deeper, higher, and farther than they have yet experienced. It is only by the grace that comes by FAITH in CHRIST that we will be able to accomplish His will in this earth.

CONTENTS

ACKNOWLEDGMENTS

*To our heavenly Father and His wonderful love.

*To our Lord, Savior and Master —Jesus Christ, who saved us and set us free because of His great love for us.

*To the Holy Spirit, who leads and guides us into the realm of miraculous living every day.

*To all of those who had a part in helping us get this book ready for the publishers.

*To my Wife Kathleen and our precious children, Michael, Daniel, Steven, Stephanie, Catherine Yu, who is our precious daughter-in-law, and Naomi, who is now with the Lord!

Introduction

The miraculous happenings, heavenly visitations, and divine deliverance's that you are about to read are all true. They have happened personally to my family and I. These experiences are recalled and shared to the best of our ability.

By no means do the following stories account for all the visitations and miracles of God that we have experienced in our lives. If we would recount every single answer to prayer, and every wonderful miracle and blessing, there would be no end to this book! Both my wife and I, including our children, have had numerous supernatural dreams, visions, healing s and experiences. In some of our heavenly encounters, God gave us specific information which has come to pass, as well as visions and dreams which have yet to be fulfilled.

What we are about to share with you in this book are simply some highlights of what we have experienced in the Lord. Some of these experiences will seem to be incredulous, however,

they are true. This is not a testimony of how spiritual we are, but how wonderful and marvelous the Father, the Son, and the Holy Ghost are! We share these experiences to the best of our recollections and understanding. Not every conversation we share in these experiences are exactly word for word. We would love to name every person that was a part of these wonderful occurrences, but privacy laws do not allow this. If you are reading this book and you saw, experienced, or were a part of these events, please do not be offended because your names were not mentioned.

At the end of this book there will be a brief teaching on how you can enter into a position where God will supernaturally begin to speak, lead and guide you in your life. It is God's will that all who follow Him would enter into this realm where all things are possible. What God has done for us, He will do for everyone. He is not a respecter of people.

GOD Said: You Better Not Lie, or You'll Die to!

One day I picked up a book by a well-known author. This book had come highly recommended by one of my favorite preachers at that time. The topic was about angelic visitations. This was something I was interested in, because of my many experiences with the supernatural. I began to read this book, and noticed immediately that there were experiences he said he had, which did not seem to line up with the Scriptures. I did not want to judge his heart, but we do have the responsibility to examine everything in light of God's Word. If it does not line up with the word of God, then we must reject it, no matter who wrote it.

As I was pondering the stories in this book, the Spirit of the Lord spoke to my heart very strongly. It was as if He was standing right there next to me, speaking audibly. What He spoke to me was rather shocking! The Lord told me that the writer of this book would be dead in three months from a heart attack. I asked the Lord why He was telling me this. He said the stories in the man's book were exaggerated, and judgment was coming. The Lord warned me that day that if I were ever to do the same thing, judgment would come to me. I did not realize that the Lord would have me to be writing books, many them filled with my own personal experiences. Now I know why he spoke this to me, telling me that I better not exaggerate my experiences.

When the Spirit of the Lord spoke this to me, I turned and told my wife. I held the book up and said, in a very quiet whispering, trembling, wavering voice, "Honey, the man who wrote this book will be dead in three months from a heart attack." Plus, I told her why the Lord told me this. I wish I had been wrong. Exactly 3 months later, the man died from a heart attack. God can speak to us through the positive and the negative circumstances of life. We better take heed to what he is saying

Dr Michael H Yeager

CHAPTER ONE

#1 An Angel & a 12 Gauge Shotgun (1969)

When I was approximately 13 years old, I went through a special program on gun safety for teenagers. If you completed this course, the state of Wisconsin would grant young teenagers the right to hunt alone. That meant that I could go out into the woods with a rifle without parental guidance. Of course, going to a special training class for gun safety does not necessarily produce maturity, which was one thing that I was seriously lacking at the time.

One early morning, my father and I got up early to go hunting. There was a layer of snow on the ground and it was quite cold. Because of this, I dressed with extra layers of clothes in order to stay warm. When we finally got to the land where we were going to go hunting, my father positioned me in the woods right next to an open field with scrub brush and small trees. He then pointed out to me where he was going to go and hunt.

He told me that I needed to stay put no matter what, until he came back to get me. He informed me that because he knew where I was at that time, if he heard me shoot, then he would come running. This particular morning, he had given me his old 12-gauge shotgun, loaded with deer slugs.

All that morning I stood very still where my father had placed me, scanning the horizon looking for deer. As the day progressed, the temperature began to rise. Before the day had progressed very far, the snow that had been on the ground had melted away. It was going from one extreme to another. It was very cold in the morning when we first went out, but now it was getting quite warm. Of course I had too many clothes on for this type of weather which was making me quite miserable. I was just too hot. I had on my hunting jacket, a hunter's hat, my orange vest, winter boots and insulated pants. Plus, I had no water with me or anything else to keep me cool.

It's hard to believe the next thing that I did. It was extremely stupid. There must have been divine angelic protection and deliverance even though I did not know Christ at the time nor was I right with God. Thank the Lord for His mercy, long-suffering, kindness and goodness towards sinners!

My dad's old 12-gauge shotgun was actually too large and heavy for me. I had been holding it all that morning which was hurting my arms. So what did I do? I sat the stock of the rifle down into the brush next to me. The barrel was aimed towards the heavens. Unbeknownst to me was the fact that there was a small briar patch at my feet that I had stuck the stock of my gun into.

I stood there for quite a while just looking around for possible deer. As time went on, I began to get tired of standing. The next thing that I did was even more stupid than the first. I decided to lean on the barrel of the gun. I mean, I literally took the barrel of the gun and put it under my armpit. The barrel of the gun was aimed in the pit of my arm. If it were to go off, the deer slug would pass up through my chest and out through my head. I would be a headless corpse. I put all of my weight on this gun barrel because I had grown extremely tired of standing.

Now, the next thing that I want to share with you is extremely amazing. There was absolutely no wind on this particular day. The gun stock was stuck in the briar patch with a branch that was inserted into the trigger guard. Of course, I did not know at the time that a branch was pushing up against the trigger which, if fired, would have taken off my chest and my head, killing me instantly. I would have gone immediately to hell because I did not know Christ.

So, as I'm leaning on the top of the barrel of the 12 gauge, I literally felt someone behind me flip the hat off the top of my head. I mean it literally felt like somebody took their finger and knocked that hat right off my head from the back to the front. Remember, there was no wind blowing whatsoever. The instant that my hat was knocked off my head, I leaned forward to get it as it was falling towards the ground. There was no wind blowing as I stated earlier. There is no reason why my hat should have fallen off. The second that I leaned forward, the barrel of this 12 gauge shotgun was no longer under my armpit. It was just inches away from my body behind my back. As soon as the barrel of the gun was out from underneath my armpit, the twig that was in the trigger guard pulled the trigger. I heard and felt a loud BANG!!!

The gun had gone off on its own. I stood there trembling and shaking knowing that it was a miracle that I was still alive. That 12-gauge deer slug would have taken my head off. God had rescued my sorry soul. I am absolutely convinced that the Lord had sent an angel or even my own guardian angel to rescue me. I believe that this angel took his little finger and flipped my hat off my head knowing that the trigger of my gun was going to be squeezed at any moment by a small branch. A little bit later my dad came by. I never did tell him or anyone else what had happened that day. Beyond any shadow of doubt I know that I would be dead if God had not rescued me.

Romans 2:4 Or despisest thou the riches of his goodness and forbearance and longsuffering; not knowing that the goodness of God leadeth thee to repentance?

#2 Saving a Barracks Full of Sleeping Men (1973)

This happened before I was even born again. Back in the late summer of 1973 after I had completed my boot camp at Great Lakes Naval base, I was moved to a training center to become an electrician's mate at a nearby military base. One night as I was peaceably sleeping at about 3 AM in the morning I smelt smoke. Now this in itself was amazing because my sense of smell was almost nonexistent. My nose had been broken at least three times if not four. The worst time was when I had been knocked to the ground, and a guy who was quite a bit bigger than me, took his right foot and slammed it right down onto my face, crushing my nose.(God healed me of this condition in 1975).

My sense of smell at this time was completely gone, and yet here I was smelling smoke. A sense of urgency hit my heart as I smelled the smoke, and I jumped up immediately out of my bunk. I slipped on my pants, and headed out to try to find out where the smoke was coming from. It was like my heart was possessed with an extreme urgency to get up and move. I approached the man who was standing guard duty at the entrance to our barracks, asking him if he smelled any smoke? He informed me that he did not smell smoke whatsoever. I decided that I needed to walk around outside and see if I could find out what was going on.

This action was highly unusual for me because I was usually in my own little world, being a total slacker. The only thing I cared about was getting drunk and getting high. Now here I was with this sense of urgency to find out where the smell of smoke was coming from. This had to be God moving upon my heart even before I was born again. I walked around to the back side of our barracks looking as I went to see where the smoke was coming from. Right behind our barracks was another barracks approximately five story high. Immediately I saw that smoke was pouring out of a window on the second (or was it the third?) floor. I ran towards the barracks, past the guard who had fallen asleep. I ran to the nearest fire alarm, grabbing it and pulling it as I ran past.

The next 20 minutes or so were busy as other men joined me in evacuating all of the men from the barracks, and fighting the fire. God must have supernaturally enhanced my sense of smell, and then gave me a great sense of urgency so that he could save those men in that barracks. I did receive a letter from the commanding officer, the Admiral of the base, thanking me for my quick thinking, response, and heroics of my action on that day saving the lives of my fellow sailors.

Every circumstance whether of God or of the devil is an opportunity for us to walk by faith. It is extremely important in the day and hour that we are living in to be directed and led by the Holy Ghost every moment. What comes to us does not make us or break us, but it is how we respond to the circumstances that would determine the outcome. Those around us can be full of hate and bitterness, but we needed to be full of the divine love of Christ. The spiritual principle that we reap what we sow is in operation whether we believe it or not.

Luke 6:38 Give, and it shall be given unto you; good measure, pressed down, and shaken together, and running over, shall men give into your bosom. For with the same measure that ye mete withal it shall be measured to you again.

#3 I drove the Alcan freeway in Winter   (Dec 1974)
Angelic Protection on the Alcan Highway!

The Alaska Highway (also known as the Alaska-Canadian Highway, or Alcan Highway) was constructed during World War II for the purpose of connecting the lower U.S. to Alaska through Canada. The pioneer road was completed in 1942 and is approximately 1,680 miles (2,700 km) from Dawson Creek to Delta Junction. This road has been legendary over many decades for being a rough, challenging drive as well as being very dangerous, especially during the winter. I had the privilege of traveling this highway by myself when I was 18 years old in December of 1974. Mark it up as one of the stupidest things I could've ever done.

At the time, I was based at Adak, Alaska during my tour in the Navy. I ended up in the military hospital in Anchorage because the first time that I flew in a high-altitude jet, my left eardrum ruptured. After they replaced my eardrum, they would not allow me to fly for a given amount of time. So here I was, stuck in Anchorage with nothing to do. Then, the silly and stupid thought came into my mind to drive back to Wisconsin going down the Alcan freeway (which was still a dirt road) in my 1969 Javelin which I had just purchased. Of course by this time, snow had already fallen across Alaska and parts of Canada. To go from Anchorage to Mukwonago, Wisconsin would be close to 3500 miles. My vehicle was not designed for winter. It was a semi souped-up vehicle with side pipes and headers, racing stripes along the side.

I was 18 years old and stupid. Of course I did not ask anyone's opinion whether or not I should do this. In addition to everything, I had very little money but this thought came into my head and I could not get it out. I bought a set of snow tires for the back, putting my regular wide, slick tires on the backseat. I bought myself a map and a bit of extra supplies, then I filled up my gas tank, not really checking to make sure if any other gas stations would be open along the way. I never considered the thought of freezing to death nor of falling into a mountain ravine.

It was late in the day and snowing when I finally headed for Wisconsin. The thought of driving all the way home with bragging rights about it to my buddies was exciting. But, before long, this exciting, adventurous journey became a nightmare of 3500 miles of excruciating tiredness, danger and fear. I soon discovered that my car was not made for these kinds of roads. The Alcan freeway seemed to be more like a dirt road for logging than one made for normal traffic. I kept plugging away mile after mile, bouncing through the potholes, pushing my way through snowdrifts, driving over very scary bridges with no guard rails and praying all the way even though I was not a Christian.

After the third day of driving with no sleep, I found myself on top of a very high mountain. On my right hand side, I could see a river way down below. It was a very large river but, up on the top of this mountain, it looked very small. (When I eventually did get to the bottom I discovered that it was a very large river indeed.) There were no railings on the right-hand side of the road and there was just a large ditch on the left-hand side. The snow plow trucks must have just gone through because there were large snow banks off to my left. I was driving with my right hand and I was resting my left hand on the arm rest when, all of a sudden, I fell asleep.

I woke up with the sensation of going over a cliff. I was dead, a goner for sure because my right hand would surely have pulled the vehicle to the right, sending it down the side of the mountain. I came to a sudden stop. Opening my eyes, I discovered that I had plowed into a large snow bank to my left. By some miracle, my right hand had not pulled the vehicle to the right but had gone up over the top to the left. There was enough snow on the ground to where it cushioned my vehicle and prevented it from slamming into the side of the mountain. As I was standing outside of my vehicle wondering what to do, lo and behold, a man with a four-wheel drive Jeep drove up behind me. It was only after all of this had all transpired that I realized all of the amazing miracles that God had done for me. I am now convinced that this man was an angel because there had been no other traffic on the road. He hooked up a rope to my back end and pulled my vehicle out of the ditch.

I thanked this gentleman, got into my car, put it into gear and took off once again. After quite a distance going down the mountain, I finally entered a very long and straight stretch of road. All of a sudden, my eyes went cross and I could not get them uncrossed. I saw two roads and then I saw two electrical poles. I picked the wrong one. On the path to crash into this pole, the deep snow slowed me so much that the bumper of my vehicle just barely bumped the pole before I stopped.

To my utter amazement, the same man in the same Jeep as before was right behind me. He seemed rather strange because he never really said anything to me. He simply hooked up a rope and pulled me out of my predicament once again. I do remember him telling me that I better stop somewhere and get some sleep. I told him that I had very little money and just had enough to get to Wisconsin. He informed me that right down the road was a gentleman that had cabins where the logging crews and road workers stayed. He said their prices for a meal and a place to sleep were very reasonable.

Once again I began to drive and, sure enough, off to my right was the place he was telling me about. That night I bought the cheapest meal I could, crawled into a bunk bed in a large room with other men and got a much-needed sleep.

Many other adventures happened along this road. I made my way through complete blizzards, slid into countless ditches, yet somehow miraculously surviving and coming out the other side. For 3500 miles, God was trying to reveal Himself to me but I was not yet ready to heed. It would still be another 2 months before the Lord finally arrested me and took control of my life just as I was on the brink of suicide, knife in hand, about to slit my wrist. I believe that this journey had somewhat of an impact upon me getting saved. I think that unconsciously I was wondering where I would have spent eternity if my vehicle had gone over that mountain cliff or if I would have frozen to death. I believe that I knew in my heart of hearts that God had protected me and provided for me even though I did not know him at that time.

When I finally got to Mukwonago, Wisconsin, I had lost over 10 pounds. When I began the journey I probably only weighed about 130 pounds to begin with. It had taken me seven days to drive the 3500 miles. I believe that when I get to heaven, I will be able to look back at that journey and see the incredible number of times that God protected me while driving on the Alcan Highway!

Romans 2:4 Or despisest thou the riches of his goodness and forbearance and longsuffering; not knowing that the goodness of God leadeth thee to repentance.

#4 Under the Ice (1975)

A friend of mine by the name of Dale, with whom I had been sharing Christ with, decided to go fishing with me one day. It was the middle of winter in Alaska. Now, we are talking about being way out there on the Aleutian chain. Adak, Alaska was our naval duty station. In retrospect, it probably wasn't too brilliant to be involved in such activities at that time of the year. We walked through deep snow in the tundra, working our way towards a small lake which we knew had trout. We finally pushed our way through the deep snow and made it to a stream which we were going to have to cross. Dale said we needed to find a place that we could jump over without stepping on the ice just in case it would not hold us. I told him that I thought the ice was more than thick enough to step on.

I told Dale that I was going to show him as I stepped out onto the ice on the stream. Dale immediately encouraged me to get off of the ice, but I told him that it was perfectly solid and okay to be on. Standing in the middle of this stream, I started jumping up and down telling him, "See, it's solid." when suddenly, I broke through the ice; plunging into the freezing water. I was swallowed by the depths and dragged by the fast-moving deep stream. I literally ended up underneath the ice. I could not find the bottom of the stream. It was way over my head. The current began to pull me down stream. I was a goner —a dead man.

I could not find my way back to the hole in the ice were I had broken through. All of a sudden I felt something grab hold of me, pulling me back through the hole in the ice. After my rescue, I discovered that it was Dale. It had to be supernatural because he had been at least 15 feet away from me when I fell in, but yet he was there so quick. Dale is a tall, lanky fellow. With his long arms, he had reached underneath the ice in the direction the current was taking me and grabbed me by my parka hood. God had used him to save my life.

Psalms 22:5 They cried unto thee, and were delivered: they trusted in thee, and were not confounded.

#5 He Died Because He Did Not Heed My Warnings!

One night (back in 1975) while I was praying alone in my barracks, when a holy **unction**, and urgency came upon me to pray for a Muslim man that I knew. As I responded to this **unction** of the Holy Ghost I entered into deep travail for his soul. I began to weep almost uncontrollably for this man, whose name was Hussein. He was a military friend of mine that I used to do drugs with. As I prayed the Spirit of God spoke to my heart, telling me the devil was going to kill him in the very near future if he did not repent, and cry out to Jesus. The spirit of God told me that Hussein had only a very short period of time left on the earth before the enemy would snuff out his precious life.

This **unction**, this deep urgency of God was so strong within me that I got up off of the floor of my dorm room, where I had been praying. I immediately went to his room and knocked on his door. Hussein opened his door and saw me standing there weeping uncontrollably. I was so moved in my heart that I could not speak for a while. He asked what was wrong with great concern in his voice. "Mike, Mike, what's wrong?" I could barely speak in English because I was weeping so hard. I finally was able to tell him that I had been in prayer in my room, when the Spirit of God literally told me that the devil was about to kill him. I told him that his time to get right with the Lord was running out. I explained that he was going to be dead in the very near future, and that he would end up in hell without Jesus. I began to plead with him with great urgency and compassion, with tears flowing down my face to get right with God. I encouraged him to cry out to God, repent for his sins, and give his heart to Jesus Christ.

It was obvious the Spirit of God was moving upon him in a very real way. He said that he believed what I was saying was true, but that he just was not ready to make that kind of commitment at this time. Soon after this experience I left the Navy, headed out to minister to the Yupik Indians. I kept in touch with some of the people that I knew on this military base. It was approximately two months later that I was speaking to one of my friends on the base when he asked me if I had heard about what happened to Hussein. I informed him, no that I had not heard anything. He told me that they had discovered him dead, with his head in the toilet. They think that he had either gotten his hands on some bad drugs or he had simply overdosed. Oh how it must break the heart of God when souls are lost because they will not respond to his love and beckoning call.

#6 Preaching Jesus was about to get me pulverized!

There was a big Texan I knew in the Navy who actually rode bulls in rodeos at one time. We called him Tuck, to this day I don't know why. After I gave my heart to **Jesus Christ**, I shared the gospel with him, his friends, and as many as I could. The Spirit of the Lord had begun to move upon one of Tuck's friends. Tuck was extremely irritated at me for causing this man to come under conviction. Up until the time I had given my heart to **Jesus**, tuck had been a good friend of mine. But now that I was in love with **Christ**, he did not want anything to do with me. Whenever he looked at me it was with great disdain.

One-night Tuck came into my room completely intoxicated with alcohol. He woke me up banging on my door like a madman. I went out to see what he wanted. When I entered the foyer he grabbed me by the neck with his large left hand. He literally picked me up off the floor by my neck and slammed me against the wall. He clenched his right hand into a fist right in front of my face pulling it back as if getting ready to hit me with all of his might. His fist literally was as big as my face. He told me that he was going to pulverize me if I did not promise to leave one of his drinking buddies alone. The man he was speaking about had taken an interest in the gospel.

In the natural, my heart should have been filled with great fear because without a shadow of a doubt he could easily beat me to death. I could literally see, and feel the devil in him. His face was all red, and his steely blue eyes were bulging, but instead of fear what rose up in my heart was a great compassion for his soul. Right there on the spot as I was hanging from my neck with his hand pinning me against the wall I began to weep for him. I told him that he could do whatever he wanted to do to me, but I would never stop preaching and exalting **Jesus Christ**. I told him that I loved him and he needed to get right with God.

He began to shake violently like a leaf in a strong wind. His fist was moving back and forth in front of my face. His mouth was moving erratically with foam coming between his teeth and hanging on his lips. During this time the other men in my barracks had heard the commotion and were all standing around watching this event unfold. After what seemed a long time Tuck finally lowered his fist and put me down. He turned around without a word and walked away from me. From that moment up until I left the Navy he never spoke to me again.

Many years later I was talking with Willie, the cowboy. Willie had become a master chief in the Navy and his expertise was underwater demolition. I asked what had happened to Tuck. Right after that event with me he said, Tuck lost his mind. He literally took his Colt 44 magnum pistol and walked up to our militaries base commander and put the gun against his head.

Thank God he did not shoot the man, but of course he was arrested and court-martialed. Tuck ended up being an alcoholic which caused him to lose his wife and family, and then he was diagnosed with cancer. Now the story does have a wonderful ending. Willie the cowboy told me that during his time in the Navy with me he really was not right with God. But the spirit of God had arrested him, and he had gotten right with **Jesus**. Willy the cowboy had stayed in contact with Tuck all of those years and eventually had a chance to speak to him about the Lord. Before Tuck died Willie had the opportunity to lead Tuck to **Christ**, he was gloriously born again; shortly thereafter, Tuck died and went home to be with the Lord. Someday, Lord willing, I will see him again. Only this time we will have sweet fellowship.

CHAPTER TWO

#7 When I slit my Artery (1975)

The next day I was in my barracks working on some of my fishing equipment. My roommate, Dale, and I were going to go fishing again. I had purchased a small plastic box with all kinds of fishing lures in it. I went to open it but no matter what I did, it would not open. That box was just downright stubborn. Then, a brilliant idea came to my mind (that was actually quite stupid). I went to my dresser, opened the top drawer and pulled out my survival knife. This was the same knife which I had bought previously with the intention of slitting my wrist in order to kill myself. Thank God the Spirit of the Lord fell upon me and gave me a revelation that I would go to hell. This caused me to fall to my knees and cry out to Jesus!

Picture this knife. It was approximately one-foot-long, and on the very end of the handle, there was a cap that you could screw off in order to store matches and other small, useful things for used for wilderness survival. Believe me when I tell you that this knife was extremely sharp. I had this brilliant idea that I could use the tip of this knife to pry open the lid of this stubborn, plastic box. So, brilliant me held this box between my thumb and little finger.

Immediately I perceived that I was going to get in trouble. The box was too close to my palm, so I moved it even further away, to the very tip of my thumb and my pinky. I began to apply pressure to the tip of the knife by pushing downward. This little box just did not want to open! I began to apply a lot more pressure and, as I did, the box slipped from between my pinky and my thumb. Now, here's the problem; the blade of the knife was aimed downwards towards my hand. When the box slipped, the blade of the knife came down and sliced me from the wrist to the beginning of my thumb. It cut through my flesh like a hot knife through soft butter. It went so deep that it literally cut through an artery. If you would open an anatomy book that shows the human circulatory system, you would discover that near your wrist, on the thumb side, is a major artery called the radial artery. The instant that I cut through this artery, it seemed as if blood shot so high that it could have hit the 8-foot ceiling above my head.

This was back in 1975 so maybe my memory is a little bit blurry. I'm not really quite sure. All I know is that the blood began to gush. I immediately applied pressure to the cut with my right hand. Thank God that Dale was in the room doing something else. Remember, Dale had just rescued me from drowning the day before. I yelled out to him, "Dale, Dale!" causing him turn around. His face immediately turned an ashen white. I told him, "I need to get to the hospital!" Our barracks were located on the top of a very high hill; the hospital was down in the valley.

Here we were in Adak, Alaska with snow piled 5 feet deep everywhere. The roads were clear to some extent but it was extremely slippery outside. There was no traffic on the road because there was a small blizzard blowing through. Dale's car was a small Volkswagen Beetle that was all beat up. The incident was somewhat hilarious though, because Dale was losing it like a newlywed husband whose wife was about ready to give birth to their first baby at any moment.

He put my winter coat over my shoulders because I could not stick my hand through the arm sleeve. There was blood beginning to spread everywhere. As I was keeping pressure to the severed artery, Dale opened up the car door for me to get in once we were out to his car. He then closed the door and ran to his side. He started that old Volkswagen up. The engine was cold, causing it to clack away in close to 20° below zero weather. When the engine finally smoothed out to some extent, he put it in reverse, backing out of this parking space.

Then, off he went! I'll never forget that ride. It's a miracle we made it to the hospital. We were going down the mountain like a toboggan with a madman in the front. I kept telling him, "Dale, slow down, you're going to get us killed!" He would whip around those mountain curves, narrowly missing going over the edge. Thank God for the high snow banks because we hit them repeatedly. If you could have seen this, we would've looked like Laurel and Hardy because Dale was so tall and I was so short, but fortunately I wasn't fat. Miracles of miracles, we finally arrived at the hospital. When I went into the emergency room, there was nobody in front of us. Of course they had to use quite a number of stitches in my hand and wrist in order to seal up the artery. As a result of this stupid accident, I now have a large scar on the palm of my hand, next to my thumb. To this day, I have a limited range of motion in my thumb, plus it certainly doesn't like the cold weather. But, believe you me, I am not complaining because I know that God rescued me once again from my stupidity. Thank God for his mercy!

#8 A Gang Leader Kept Trying to Stab Me to Death

After being born again for a while, I perceived in my heart that I needed to reach out and witness to the gang I used to run with right outside of Chicago. We were not a gang in the sense that we had a name or any entrance rituals that we had to go through. We were just a group of young men who were constantly involved in corruption, drinking, fighting, using drugs, stripping cars, and doing other things to horrible that I will not mention. One day, I was sitting in a car between the two instigators of most of our shenanigans, Gary and Claire. Both of these men were very large and quite muscular.

I had fervently shared Christ with them and the others to let them know how much God had changed me. They sat around drinking, using dope, and cussing while I shared the good news with them. I explained I was on a heavenly high that drugs and the world could never take them to. Most of them just stared at me, not knowing how to respond. They all had known the old Mike Yeager. The crazy and ungodly stuff that I had done. They had seen me many times whacked out on drugs and alcohol. Now here I was a brand-new creation in Christ preaching Jesus with a deep and overwhelming zeal.

Now Gary who was one of the main leaders was different in many negative ways than the other guys. He was like a stick of dynamite ready to explode at any moment. He had been up to the big house already and spent some time behind the bars of justice. He never did like me, but now there was an unspoken, seething hatred for me under the surface, which eventually exploded. We were coming out of Racine, Illinois, as Gary was driving the car we were in. Claire was sitting against the door on the right side in the front seat, with me in the middle. At that moment I did not realize why they had put me in the middle, but it became very obvious.

Before I knew it, Gary reached up and grabbed a large knife from the dashboard of the car. I believe the vehicle was an old Impala that had the old-style steel dashboard. The heating and air conditioning were controlled by sliders in the dash. The knife had been shoved down into one of the slots. He pulled the knife out of the dashboard with his right hand, jabbed it high up into the air, and drove it down toward me very fast, trying to stab me in the gut with this knife. I saw him reach for the knife, and at that very moment I entered into the realm of the Spirit when time seems to come to a standstill. This has happened to me on numerous occasions in such dangerous situations.

When I enter this realm, time slows down while my speed or movement seems to increase. You could argue whether I speed up or time slows down. I really can't say, though; it just happens.

The knife came down toward my guts in slow motion, and I saw my hands reaching up towards the knife and grabbing Gary's wrist to prevent him from stabbing me through the gut. I could not prevent the knife from coming down, but I was able to cause it to plunge into the seat instead. His thrust had been so powerful that the knife literally pierced all the way down through the Springfield car seat. He immediately pulled it out of the car seat and tried to stab me again. He continued to try to stab me as he was driving down the road. Every time he tried to stab me, I was able to divert the stab just fractions of an inch away from my privates and for my legs.

During this entire event the peace of God was upon me in an overwhelming way. I was not shaking or breathing hard in the least; neither was my heart beating fast. It sounds unbelievable, I know, but it felt as if I were in heaven. The presence and the peace of God was upon me in a powerful supernatural way. I know this might sound extremely strange and weird, but I was actually kind of enjoying myself as I was watching God deliver me from this madman. During this entire time, it was like a slow-motion review of a movie. Up and down the knife came as he kept on trying to kill me. This large muscular man was not able to kill a small 5'8" skinny guy. I just love how God does the supernatural miracles. There was not one thing in my life in which that I knew I was out of God's will. I believe if I had been out of the will of God most likely Gary would've succeeded in murdering me. He kept on trying to kill me until up ahead of us a police car came out from a side road. Gary's car window was open and when he saw the policeman he threw the knife out the window.

Gary continued to drive down the road without ever saying a word about what had just happened. In this whole situation Claire who I had thought was a friend of mine, did not in any way try to help me. No one said a word as we drove down the road, but the peace of God was upon me like I have the invisible blanket.

Thou wilt keep him in perfect peace, whose mind is stayed on thee: because he trusteth in thee. Trust ye in the LORD forever: for in the LORD JEHOVAH is everlasting strength (Isaiah 26:3-4).

#9 Shooting to Kill

About two days later I had to go to Gary's house. I really shouldn't have gone there, because there was just something satanic and evil about him. Just the day before, he tried to stab me to death! When I pulled up in my sister's red Maverick he was sitting on his porch. When he saw me get out of the car he grabbed a shotgun (I think it was a twelve gauge) which had been leaning against his house.

I walked toward him and he aimed it right at my stomach. What was there about my gut that he was so enamored by it? There was no fear in my heart at the least. I just kept walking toward him. I was about twenty feet away from him when the barrel of the gun jerked slightly to the right as the gun went off. The sound of the gun echoed through the valley. Nothing happened to me! As I think back to that day, I firmly believe an angel nudged that gun barrel with his little finger. If there was bird shot in the gun, no pellets hit me, and if there was a deer slug in it, I did not feel it go by.

It must have missed me by a matter of inches. I was not shaking or breathing hard in the least; neither was my heart beating fast. It sounds unbelievable, I know, but once again it felt as if I was in heaven. I walked up the steps of the porch and walked up to Gary. I took the gun out of his hand, and leaned it back against the house. Gary just stared at me without saying a word. That was the last time I ever saw Gary. I have no idea what happened to him.

No weapon that is formed against thee shall prosper; and every tongue that shall rise against thee in judgment thou shalt condemn. This is the heritage of the servants of the LORD, and their righteousness is of me, saith the LORD (Isaiah 54:17).

#10 About to Drown in the Bering Sea (Jul 1975)

In this particular instance, I was underway with a captain on a fishing boat. We were in the Bering Sea, out in Bristol Bay, right off the coast from Dillingham, Alaska. We were gillnet fishing for salmon on a 40-foot vessel with only a two-man crew on this particular day. The winds were blowing, whitecaps were everywhere and the sea was pretty rough. So far, we had not taken in a lot of salmon but enough; nothing to complain about.

We then received a report over the radio that another fishing vessel was in trouble. They had run into a school of fish with their hydraulic system broken down. You see, these vessels have large hydraulic drums on the stern of the boats that are used to assist in pulling in the net filled with salmon. If these hydraulic systems break down, it puts the fishermen in great jeopardy of losing their catch, net and livelihood. If the nets got too full before they were able to pull the fish in, the net or lines could snap, resulting in losing the fish and/or the net and possibly even the end of their fishing business.

My captain informed me of the situation. He told me that we were not very far from this man and his crew. I asked them to radio this captain to see if he could use some help. This captain responded that they absolutely needed help. Since our nets were not in the water at the time, I asked my captain if he would let me go help them. He agreed to this request so we headed off into their direction. We spotted the boat with its crew frantically trying to pull in the fish before they lost everything. The captain maneuvered us as close to the vessel as he could on the rough seas with me having to take a chance and leaping over.

One of the crew was waiting for me as I leapt, grabbing me as I began to fall backwards, pulling me safely on board. Immediately, I headed to the stern of the boat where I began to grab the net, helping the other men pull the net with the fish on board their vessel. Hundreds of large salmon were in this net. They truly had come across a big school of them. We kept working nonstop as our arms, hands, legs and backs were pressed to their limit. But we could not stop, for if we did, we would lose all of the catch and the netting.

In the process of aggressively pulling their nets in, I tore and lacerated my hands open from the net, filling the wounds with fish oil, scales and slime. After this incident, my hands swelled up to almost twice their normal size. My hands became all bloated and infected, full of pain and stiffness. I'm not complaining about that day. What I did needed to be done. I'm simply saying what happened. My captain had pulled his vessel off a distance so that there would be no danger of the two vessels colliding together and causing a major incident.

It seemed like it was forever before we were finally able to pull the rest of the net in with the fish. For a while, I simply collapsed on the deck trying to get my breath and my strength back. During this time, the rough seas had not quieted down or become less violent. They were actually rougher than before. The captain on board the vessel I was on called my captain informing him that I was ready to be picked up. There were only two problems: number one he could not get real close and number two I was extremely weak. When he finally got as close as he could, I made my leap. Unfortunately, I was too tired and I fell smack dab into the Bering Sea and no, I did not have a life vest on. So here I am, in the Bering Sea, so tired I can hardly swim, caught between the two vessels where I could easily be squashed. My captain was not able to help me because he had to keep his hands on the helm. The men on the other boat cast me a line as I was trying to stay afloat and not drown.

The water was freezing; my arms and legs were cramping and man, was I ever tired. But thank God, they eventually were able pull me back onto their vessel. Once again, my captain came alongside in order to give me another opportunity to board my vessel. I waited until it seemed like both boats were in sync with the waves, then with all my strength, I leapt again. Unbelievably, once again I missed. I fell into the Bearing Sea to be plummeted by the whitecaps and the waves. I was so tired; I could hardly move my arms to keep afloat. A thought came to my mind, "What a way to die, helping another man bring in his catch." I just did not see how I was going to survive.

The men kept yelling at me to hold on until they finally tossed the rope to me again. Once again I grabbed it with all my might as they pulled me up slowly but surely onto their vessel. What was I going to do now? I was tired, weary, wet and cold with hypothermia beginning to set in. I know this sounds crazy but my captain wanted me to try once more. So, after I had a little rest, he once again maneuvered into a position as close as he dared to get. The last time the vessels were so close, I thought that I was going to be crushed between them.

This time, he tried to get even closer, risking damaging or sinking the boats. I summoned all of the strength and the energy that I had remaining and leapt with all of my might from the edge of the fishing vessel, through the air, through wind and salty sea to finally landed on the other vessel. What a day! God had rescued me once again, saving my hide to live another day. He saved me to be a fisher of men, not of fish. This was back in 1975. For over 38 years I have been fishing and, by God's grace, I will never stop being a fisher of men!

#11 Shoot the Indians

As I share some of my experiences living with the Yupik Indians, I do not want to paint a negative image of these precious people. My time with them was challenging, to say the least. I also saw that alcohol is a major tool of the devil being used to destroy their lives. There is much hurt and resentment among the Yupik Indians due to what they perceive to be a robbery of their natural resources and land from the "white man". Here I was, a young "white man", trying to reach them for Jesus Christ.

I lived, fished and hunted with them. My love and my faith was sorely tried and challenged by the young men. They treated me with total contempt and disdain. They would feed me the worst parts of their hunts. One time, after we had finished hunting, they gave me duck head, duck feet and duck guts, which I ate with no complaints and a thankful heart.

Over and over God had protected me when, at times, the natives had gone out of their way to try to do me harm. I do not blame them. I truly believe they did not know what they were doing. One time I had gone up a very wild river with some of the men my age. This trip did not turn out very well because, as we were trying to advance beyond a set of rapids two days up the river, the prop hit some rocks. It sheared the prop right off of the motor shaft. The only option we had was to float down the river until we got back to the village. Two days later, as we were floating down the river, we came across a small graveyard of abandoned boats and engines.

I suggested that we paddle over to them and look just in case we might find an old propeller that would fit our engine. Amazingly, we found a four prop blade with only one prop missing. It was the right blade to put on the boat engine. We fixed it and off we went, headed back to the village. A couple of hours later, we accidentally got too close to a sand bar and ended up stuck. They demanded that I get out of the boat and push them off the sandbar, which I did willingly. I was the only white man in their village besides a teacher.

The minute they were off the sandbar, the native who had control of the kicker (that's what they called the motor) revved the engine and took off leaving me behind. We were miles and miles from any habitation. Even their village was only accessible by river or by bush plane. My rifle was in the boat so I had no protection from the grizzlies or any of the other critters that inhabited the wilderness. All I could do was cry out to God for his divine protection. Actually, I thank God my gun was in the boat because, unbeknownst to them, I had come to the breaking point. I think that I might have been tempted to pop a couple holes in the hull of their boat with my rifle.

I followed the river for quite a distance walking back towards where I knew the village would be miles away. When I came around the corner of one bend, thank God, they were there waiting for me! They just kept pushing me to see if I would break, feeding me all of the filth from their killings, the parts of the animal that nobody in their right mind would eat. But I ate them by faith because I knew this was a test and their souls were more important to me than what my mind, stomach or taste buds were telling me. It was only the divine Spirit of God that caused me not to break under all of this pressure.

James 1:2-4[2] My brethren, count it all joy when ye fall into divers temptations; [3] knowing this, that the trying of your faith worketh patience. [4] But let patience have her perfect work, that ye may be perfect and entire, wanting nothing.

#12 Yupik Indians Tried to kill me by Steaming Me Alive (1975)

At the time that I was with the Yupik Indians it did not seem as if I had many results. However, the Word of God never returns void. I have been told by reliable sources that one of the young men I shared Jesus with is now an Assemblies of God pastor in the Dillingham area. When I was there, there was no Christian testimony in the community. But now there is an Assembly of God church right outside of Dillingham, Alaska. Now to the story of how I was almost steamed to death.

Steam baths were introduced to Yupik Indians by Russian fur traders and missionaries. The steam baths I experienced in the Bristol Bay area consisted of a dressing room, combination cooling room, and the hot room with very low ceilings that were only about four feet high. They were covered over with tundra to keep the steam and heat from escaping. These hot rooms were called a maqili or McQay.

The wood stove heater was an oil drum on its side with a chimney. Rocks were piled on top of the oil drum. There was half of a steel barrel full of water in the corner of the room next to the exit. They had about four-and-a-half-foot long piece of wood with a kitchen pan attached so they could scoop water out of the barrel, stretch the pan over the top of the oil barrel stove and dump it on the rocks. This sent forth a tremendous amount of heat and steam. They packed the barrel completely full of wood for a steam bath. Steam baths seem to be an area of great pride for the Yupik men.

They told stories how they would pass out trying to outdo each other. They were known to have fallen on the rocks and burned to death. They stayed in the steam bath as long as they could and then go out and roll in the snow or jump in the river. They also had a bench right outside where we would sit with nothing but a washcloth covering our loins.

One day they invited me to take a steam bath with them. On that particular day there were three young Yupik Indians and an older man who looked like a walrus. The Spirit of the Lord spoke to my heart and told me not to be fearful. They were going to try to steam me out of the maqili /McQay. God said not to be concerned because He was going to reveal Himself to them through this test. When we were all in the McQay and had closed the door they all stared at me, speaking in their native tongue to one another and laughing. Then they dumped water on the red hot rocks.

The older gentleman had control of the scoop. As he continued to splash water on the rocks, it began to get extremely hot. I had a wet rag which they had given me, along with a pan of water at my feet. I dipped the cloth into the water and put it against my face and nostrils. I bowed my head and prayed quietly in tongues. I could hear the water hissing as more and more water was thrown on the red hot rocks. I could feel their eyes staring at me. The heat was almost unbearable.

The minute I stopped thinking about Jesus and praying it would feel like I was being steamed alive. Finally, I heard the door of the McQay open and close three times. At this point I looked up and there was only the old Yupik Indian and myself. He smiled at me with a toothless grin. I bowed my head once again and continued to pray knowing this was going to get extremely difficult. I knew this was a fight for their souls. I wanted the Spirit of God to reveal Himself to them. They needed to understand this was not a white man's religion but Jesus is the living God and Savior of all men. All at once I heard a very large splash. The old Yupik Indian threw a whole scoop of water upon the rocks and ran out the door of the McQay.

I panicked. It felt like my flesh was being melted from off my bones. I ran for the door to open it, but either it was locked or they were holding it shut from the outside. I pounded on the door and at that instant the Spirit of the Lord arrested me and told me to go back into prayer.

I fell on my face directly on the wood plank floor and began to speak in tongues. The Spirit of God sent a cool breeze where there was no wind. A cold wind literally blew over the top of me. After what seemed to be a long time they let me out. I am sure they never understood how I could have beaten them at their own native hobby, or how I survived such tremendous heat. They never did ask me. They simply stared at me when I came out.

James 1:2 My brethren, count it all joy when ye fall into divers temptations; 3 knowing this, that the trying of your faith worketh patience. 4 But let patience have her perfect work, that ye may be perfect and entire, wanting nothing.

CHAPTER THREE

#13 The Perfect Storm (1975)

In the spring of 1975, I had fulfilled my responsibility to the US Navy! I had spent almost 3 years on an island called Adak, in Alaska. After I was dismissed from the Navy I ended up living with the Yupik Indians in the area around Dillingham Alaska. During that time, I was able to make a trip back to Adak, Alaska to visit those I had grown close to after I was born again. In order to get back to Adak, I made contact with the flying Tigers, asking them if I could hitch a ride with them. They were contracted with the US military to haul cargo and supplies to the Aleutian Islands.

Flying with the Flying Tigers to numerous islands was an experience in itself. We flew very close to the Bering Sea, just right above the icebergs. I think the reason for this was to prevent ice from forming on the wings. It was very beautiful, and yet to some extent frightening. There is no room for errors, because if our plane went down in these waters hypothermia would have set in almost immediately. I was also amazed at the meals that they fed us on our journey. Whenever we landed at an island, they had prepared for us fresh vegetables, salmon, King crabs and wonderful dishes. One thing that can be said about the flying Tigers is that they know how to treat their pilots and workers.

Eventually we landed at Adak, Alaska where I connected backup with the wonderful Christians that I had come to know and love on the island. I was informed that if I wanted to I could go on a caribou hunt with the captain of the base, the chief over the military police (which was a friend of mine) and other military men. I had brought my 357 Magnum pistol, my Winchester 270 rifle, Alaskan Fur Mukluks, Silver Fox snow hood, Military Magnesium Snowshoes. I looked more like a Yupik Indian then a Caucasian! Of course I said Yes that I would love to join this hunting trip!

Now caribou on Adak Island combines the pursuit of one of North America's finest big-game trophies with one of the most unique hunting environments in the country. Adak caribou come from a genetic stock that produces huge antlers that would make the average hunter crazy with excitement. The island itself has no predators, so Adak caribou have little to do besides getting fat and growing huge antlers. To say that Adak caribou are unique is an understatement in the extreme. The caribou were introduced to Adak Island in 1958 and 1959, by the Alaska Department of Fish and Game with approximately 200 caribou to help prevent emergency famine and recreational hunting opportunities for military personnel living there.

Our main trans port was a 110-foot military tug boat. This military tugboat was wonderful as long as there were not rough seas. Military tugboats are not made for the open ocean, but were designed for the harbors to bring in submarines and large ships. We took this tugboat around the other side of Adak Alaska to where a large caribou herd had been spotted by one of our scouts. Adak Island is an island close to the western extent of the Aleutian Islands in Alaska. The island has a land area of 274.59 square miles, measuring 33.9 miles on length and 22 miles on width, making it the 25th largest island in the United States.

Due to harsh winds, frequent cloud cover, and cold temperatures, vegetation is mostly tundra (grasses, mosses, berries, low-lying flowering plants) at lower elevations. There were some very large mountains on Adak, including and in active volcano. Adak is snow covered the greater part of the year. Very strong gales occur in all months of the year at Adak with the greatest chance from December through March. A peak gust of 125 miles an hour wind occurred at Adak in March 1954.

Our journey to the other side of the island on the tugboat was pretty much uneventful. The hunting was extremely good, with a number of very large caribou taken. I had an opportunity to shoot some caribou, but simply pass them up not knowing what I would be doing with 400 to 700 pounds of caribou being a single person. After a couple days of hunting, we all met back at the tugboat to take us back to the main base.

As we headed back out to sea, a very strong wind began to blow contrary to the direction we were going. The waves of the Bering Sea began to buck and roll in a very frightening fashion, and it felt as if we were on a wild bucking horse. It was like the sea had become angry, furious, and hungry for the destruction of our vessel. Humongous waves relentlessly pounded against our military tugboat. Every which direction are tugboat began tilt. From front to back, and from side to side. It seemed like as if times are diesel smoke stacks were going to hit the Bering Sea from left to right. The waves felt like battering rams against the hull, slamming violently against every part of the vessel. The waves became so high that we lost sight of the horizon, strong, cold and bitter winds howling all around us. The roaring and pounding became so loud that it obliterated all other sounds, even the roaring of our diesel engines struggling to plow its way through the angry sea.

I became violently seasick with all of the other sailors on board. It seemed like even the oldest and saltiest Navy sailors among us were sick. The captain of the vessel told us to stay off of the deck lest we be swept overboard. Our tugboat had run into what we would call the perfect storm. I am positive that there was not one man aboard that was not crying out to God for our protection and deliverance from this terrible storm. The trip that should've taken approximately five hours, took us all day and night until the next morning. All that day and night we were being tossed to and fro, and being shook like a mouse in the mouth of a sinister and angry cat.

When we finally pulled into the harbor of our military base, we all were extremely thankful to God that we had made this journey home. I think everyone of us knew that it had to be God's divine protection That this tugboat afloat in such overwhelming wind and waves. I think it took me approximately three days to get over the terrible seasickness they had wracked my head and body during this caribou hunt. God is so merciful, loving and protecting in all of his ways.

Chief Loyd Olds perspective.

We were coming out of three arm bay in (Adams) 110 ft. tug boat. Everything was fine until we entered into the Bering sea side of the island where we hit heavy winds and rough seas with 40 to 50 ft. swells. Everyone on board was being thrown back and forth violently. At one time the tugs skipper told me everyone onboard was sick, and he himself was feeling sick too. He asked me if I could take the controls of the tug while he went below? I agreed, and he left the helm in my hands. My son brad told me that he had to go to the bathroom really bad, so I told him to hang on to the ladder railing as tight as he could, and to come right back.

When he returned he told me everyone below deck was throwing up or moaning really bad, including the tug boat skipper. I told him to hold unto the grab pipe along the bulkhead, and not let go while we were being tossed about. The waves were breaking over the bow of the 110 ft. tug boat and rolling along both sides of the boat immersing everything under water. The skipper did finally return telling me that he felt better now, and took back the controls. I was mainly concerned for my son brad, and with him getting sick, but I guess God has blessed us both so that we ended up not having motion sickness problems, for that I am very thankful. I remember Mike Yeager telling me that he did not want to go through that ever again, but not much else. Once we rounded the northern point of Adak island the sea smoothed out considerably.

#14 Living on the mud flats   (1976)

Living on the Mud Flats, in a Tent, at 50° below Zero!!!

At 19 years old, I was working in a rustic town by the name

of Dillingham, Alaska. I was a 19-year-old kid who was trying to evangelize the Yupik Indians and anybody else I could reach. All summer and into the fall I worked, fished and lived side-by-side with not just those in Dillingham but with other natives from other villages. Actually, this little town has become famous now because of Sarah and Todd Palin who go there every season to fish for salmon.

When I was in this town back in 1975 to 1976, it was a rough-and-tumble world. Dillingham was nothing but dirt roads, rustic buildings and hardy Alaskans with strapped pistols at their sides, walking around with rifles like it was still the old rugged West. I was dressed in like fashion with a .357 Magnum at my side, a 270 Winchester rifle slung over my shoulder, wolf mukluks on my feet for the winter and a silver-fox, hooded coat to complete the ensemble.

Right outside the town of Dillingham there is what was commonly called "The Mud Flats". It is an area that many natives would set their tents up to live and work from during the salmon season. At that time, I was living in a makeshift shack right outside of town on these mud flats. It was traditionally only a summertime place for those who were fishing to set up a temporary residence. Everybody had left it a long time before except for me.

I had nowhere else to stay. The winter came before I knew it. After summer, with some help, I covered a tent with plywood on the outside and with thin insulation and plywood on the inside. We had found a big old bay window with only single-paned glass and installed it in the back portion of the tent. This window faced the Nushagak River upon which Dillingham was built next to. This is where all the boat docks were located, close to the cannery.

I got myself an old 55-gallon barrel and put a wood stove pipe on one end and a door on the other where I could insert wood. In order to support myself during the wintertime, I applied for a job at one of the only gas stations at that time. They hired me to pump gas, change tires and do grunt work as required.

Before I knew what happened, winter came with her full Arctic vengeance. I'm telling you it was one cold and snowy winter. In my plywood covered tent, the wind would shake it as it blew across the mud flats. It was over 50° below outside not counting the wind-chill factor. My bed was nothing but a wooden frame with a piece of plywood. I would crawl into my sleeping bag praying and believing God that I would not freeze during the night.

I would get up the next morning in order to walk over 5 miles to work. Over 90% of the time I would never get a ride. My heart was content; however, as I would cry out to Jesus, I would ask Him for the opportunity to share the good news with anyone I met or who would listen to me. My heart yearned to win souls and to be more like Jesus every day. This cry has never left me. Here was an environment that would try the hearts and test the faith of any godly man. I want you to know that God was with me in a powerful way in this situation.

So here I was, living on the howling, freezing, lonely Mud Flats. Nobody else was there but me and Jesus. One extremely cold morning, I got up freezing. My mustache was covered with frost from my breath. I was so cold that I knew that I needed to start a fire really quick.

What I did next, I knew better but at the time it didn't concern me. I had some gasoline which I kept to help start fires. I took an old coffee can and filled it probably half-full. After I had the wood stove full of wood, I threw the gasoline onto the logs. Then I took a match and threw it into the 55-gallon drum. Of course you know what happened. It exploded, sending fire rushing out of the barrel and engulfing me head to toe! The blast was so huge that it threw me onto my back. In spite of my stupidity, God protected me. I had some singed hair on my face and head but that was the only damage.

What unforgettable and amazing adventures I had during that time of my life! I look back now and am utterly amazed at how God kept me and preserved me during those times. Thank you, Jesus, for Your wonderful protection and mercy!!!

Isaiah 43:2 When thou passest through the waters, I will be with thee; and through the rivers, they shall not overflow thee: when thou walkest through the fire, thou shalt not be burned; neither shall the flame kindle upon thee.

#15 Saved a man from bleeding to death! (1976)

In the late fall of 1975 I ended up working for a gas station in Dillingham Alaska. Basically my job was to repair tires, fill people's vehicles with gas, clean up, and do whatever was necessary. When I was 16 years old I had already worked at a gas station in my hometown of Mukwonago Wisconsin. This was the only gas station at that time available in Dillingham. One of the main roads that ran through that area from the airport to the town was still nothing but a dirt road. The name of the road was called Kanakanak which actually led to a hospital about 6 miles down. The main mechanics name was George, who was a Seventh-day Adventist, who had become a good friend of mine.

Now this gas station was basically a rundown facility, with lots of old junk vehicles parked and stacked along one side of the mechanic shop. The gas pumps probably should've been replaced many years ago. One day as I was repairing tires, George was backing up the tow truck with a vehicle connected out of the shop on to the main road. The next thing I know, I heard the sound of a collision. Being busy with the repair of a tractor-trailer tire I just kept working.

A couple minutes later George comes in telling everybody that there had just been an accident. That some young native Alaskan came whipping around the corner on the dirt road while George had the vehicle back out onto it, and this motorcycle had slammed right into the vehicle that was connected to his tow truck.

This young native who had slammed into the vehicle with his motorcycle, had gone flying through the air.

The spirit of God rose up in me. I knew in my heart at that moment I had to get to this young man because his life was in danger. I jumped away from the big semi-trailer tire that I was working on. I said to George: "Where is he right now?" He said to me, "He flew through the air and he's in the midst of all the junk vehicles." I ran out through the large garage doors and headed over to the Junkers.

As I came around the corner and began to look among the Junkers, I saw him lying on his back amidst a bunch of jagged steel. I ran over to him, noticing immediately there was blood everywhere. I jumped down into the midst of the scrap metal examining what was going on. The young man was already going into shock. I began to examine his body trying to find out where all the blood was coming from. I noticed immediately that it was from the calf of his right leg.

When he had flown through the air he had come down in the midst of very sharp metal and his leg had hit some type of sharp steel, slicing his leg calf muscles all the way to his bare bone. He must've cut an artery because blood was gushing. Immediately I tore away the remainder of the leg of his pants. I quickly pulled off my outer shirt, and made a makeshift tourniquet. During this whole time, I was not even thinking, I was just moving in the Holy Ghost. He had lost a lot of blood, and I began to speak life over him in the name of Jesus Christ of Nazareth. Once I was able to get the blood to stop flowing, I began to yell for George.

I do not know why, but nobody came to check out what was going on from the gas station. I think I was just moving in supernatural fast speed, where everything seems to slow down, and time ceases to exist. It might've been only a matter of minutes since the accident happened, but it felt like a long time to me. George heard my yelling, and came around the corner. I told him we needed to get him to the hospital right now. The only hospital around was Kanakanak Hospital.

Somehow all by myself I was able to get this young man up as George was bringing his old Jeep Wagoneer around to the front of the gas station. Now this native American was actually taller and bigger than me. He looked to be right around the same age as I was. I was able to get him into the car and onto the back seat of this old Jeep Wagoneer. As George was driving us to the hospital, I examined this man's leg more closely. It was split down the middle like an overcooked hotdog in the microwave.

You could literally see all the veins, and muscles right down to the bone. In the natural I should have been shaking and trembling, because I really do not like the sight of blood and mangled muscles. As we bounced along on the dirt road I was simply speaking life and healing. This young man was completely gone, lost in the midst of the shock and the trauma.

We finally arrived at the hospital. I was able to get him out (it had to be God) of the Jeep and into the emergency room. For some reason there were hardly any personnel there. Of course, back in those days the hospital was not very large, and very old and rustic. Finally, a young man who was training to be a doctor was able to see us. Because there is no one else there to help him, he asked if I would be willing to remain and be his assistant. There was a complete calmness and yet a divine boldness about me. I told him I would be more than willing. We were finally able to get him up onto an operating table. This young physician began to cut away more of the scraps off his pant legs. There was a headlamp light that he turned down and turned on in order to examine more carefully the damage to this man's leg.

I noticed immediately that this young physician began to shake and tremble. I know this will be hard to believe, but by the spirit of God I began to speak calmness to this young physician. I actually by the spirit of God began to tell him what he needed to do. I had absolutely no medical knowledge whatsoever, and yet at that moment I knew what needed to be done. I had to literally push together this man's leg, and its cloven separated parts, in order for it to be sewed back together.

The physician's hands were shaking like leaves in the wind as he was handling the large needle and thread. My hands were covered in blood, and yet there was not one bit of tremble in my hands. I do have to some small degree a trembling in my hands, but there was no trembling or shaking that day in my hands. There was no fear, or anxiety in my heart.

I cannot tell you exactly how long this operation took, but when it was done his leg was put back together. During this whole time, I was praying, and speaking very quietly. You do not have to get loud and boisterous when you're walking and moving by faith in the Holy Ghost. I left that young man in the hands and the care of the hospital. I do not think that I ever saw the young man again, but I still pray and hope the Holy Ghost, the residue of the spirit of the Lord that I imparted as I laid my hands upon him, is still working in him mightily.

CHAPTER FOUR

#16 God had me fly first class to prevent Death & Destruction   (1976)

I was going back to visit relatives in the lower 48, flying out from Anchorage Alaska. When I went to the airline check-in counter, I had no intentions of buying a first-class ticket. To me it was just a waste of money, but as I was standing at the counter this overwhelming unction rose up within my heart to fly home first-class. A First-class ticket of course was much more expensive than an economy ticket, but thank God I did have the money. I was not dressed to fly 1st class, seeing that I had just left Dillingham Alaska, with only the clothes on my back, and what I had in a backpack.

As they were boarding us onto the plane, a 747, they were looking at our ticket stubs. The stewardess began to direct me to those who were flying economy. I informed her that actually I had a first-class ticket. She looked at me like maybe I had lost my mind. I had to double check the ticket, and sure enough it was first-class. Back in those days' people did not dress like hobos with holes in their pants when they flew first-class. People today dress in whatever way they like, and no one thinks anything about it. She grudgingly let me go past her into the 1st class section. One of the stewardesses, whose main job was to cater to the first-class, looked at me as I walked up to her with my ticket extended from my hand. Her look spoke a thousand words, as if to say "What are you doing here you ragamuffin?"

After she looked at my ticket, she directed me to my seat. I had never flown first-class so I really did not know what the seating arrangement would be. Most aisles had four chairs in each row. Two to the left, and two to the right. But where I was directed there was only two chairs, one to the left, where the stewardess sat me down, and one to my right. Now remember this was back in 1976, so first-class is completely different now than it was then. In front of me was nothing but the bulkhead of the plane. I was literally sitting in the nose of this plane. I thought to myself, if this is first-class, it sure is not worth the money I'm paying.

After the plane was completely boarded, I discovered that there was nobody to my right. This particular seat was empty. I remember thinking something is not right, maybe I should not have bought first-class? We were headed to O'Hare airport in Chicago directly from Anchorage Alaska. It was an approximately 6 ½ hour flight. I settled down for a comfortable flight, taking a nap and reading my Bible.

We finally arrived at our final destination, but for some reason the plane was not landing. Actually they had put us into a holding pattern, and we simply kept on flying around. After what seemed to be a long time, the pilot of the plane came over the loudspeaker, informing us that there had been a technical problem. They had been trying to fix it, but with no success. They informed us that the front landing gear would not lock in place. I do remember the landing gear which was right below me for the front wheel kept on clunking and making noise. They were lifting it and lowering it over and over trying to get it to lock into place. Now imagine this, this is the 1st time I have ever flown first-class, and here I was sitting in the nose of the 747, with the front landing gear not locking in. The pilot informed us that we were going to have to land. There was no other options.

As he was speaking, the Spirit of God spoke to my heart. He said to me: "This is why you are flying 1st class right over the top of the front nose landing gear and wheel! You need to stand upon the word of God, and take authority over this situation, in order to preserve the lives of those on this plane!" I could hardly believe my spiritual ears! I said: "Really Lord?" "Yes." He instructed me to begin to pray that the front landing gear would not collapse, even though it would not be locked in place.

Since that time I have researched this situation and from my research I have discovered that if the front nose landing gear goes out, you are in big trouble, especially on a 747. From all my research it would seem that with the 747 full of people, the pressure on the front nose gear and wheel would be approximately 90,000 pounds, with the weight of the plane and the pressure of our forward motion. Approximately 9% of the whole weight of the plane would be on that wheel. The 747 weighs almost 1 million pounds fully loaded. Now that is some serious weight, and if that nose wheel collapsed, the nose of that 747 would be eating nothing but asphalt, concrete, and ground.

I quietly began to cry out to the Lord for our safe landing. I took authority over the devil and all the demonic powers behind this potential terrible tragedy. I commanded the landing gear to stay in place. There was absolutely no fear in my heart, nothing but peace, knowing now that God had put me there on purpose, not to be destroyed, but to speak his word over this situation.

As we came in for the landing, with all the landing gears extended, the flaps completely down, I could see the fire trucks and the rescue trucks, and ambulances all lined up waiting for the plane to crash. The pilot brought the speed of the 747 to the very edge of its stalling speed, with all the weight we had on board is approximately 160 miles an hour. The back wheels touched down, with the pilot trying to keep the front wheels of the nose off the ground as long as he could. Finally, the front landing wheel hit the concrete. You could feel the tension on the plane, and I'm sure there was a lot of people praying.

Thank God It Held! As the plane finally came to a stop, everybody was filled with great joy over our safe landing, never realizing that God had put at least one person in first-class, right over the top of the landing gear in order to stop the enemy from killing or destroy all the precious lives on that plane. Will I ever fly 1st class again? Only if God quickens my heart and tells me to do it again!

#17 Drunk on a motorcycle

Thank God for His wonderful mercy, kindness and goodness. Even when we fall short, He's still there to help us, protect us and to keep us. There was a brief period in my life after I gave my heart to Christ that I basically backslid. I was like a yo-yo in my walk with God for maybe two months; messing up, repenting, walking with God and then messing up again, just to start the cycle over. Everything is a little bit foggy about those particular days. I had come back to Wisconsin from being in Alaska, doing missionary work with the Yupik Indians.

Before I left Alaska, depression began to hit me hard. You see, I did not have enough depth in the Word of God. Not only that but I was not attending a good, spirit-filled Word church. There actually was no spirit filled church at that time available in Dillingham, Alaska. (I have heard from some good sources that there is now an Assembly of God church there.) I began to go into deep depression out there on the mud flats of Alaska. Here it was, the middle of winter and 40° below with the wind and the snow whipping around my little wooden shack made from a tent frame. I found myself beginning to dabble back into drugs and alcohol. I knew that I was in big time trouble, so while I still had a little money left, I bought a ticket back to my hometown in Wisconsin.

When I got back to Mukwonago, I began to try to share my faith once again. During this time, I was able to land a job in Waukesha, Wisconsin at a company that built transformers for high voltage lines. It was a very good paying job but I was completely unsatisfied. I could not find any believers. I'm talking about people who really were excited about Jesus Christ and who wanted to go all the way. I found myself beginning to visit the bars where I used to hang out.

In the beginning I was simply there to share my faith and drink a soda, but before I knew it, I was having a beer here and there. One night, I ran into an old friend who was also driving a motorcycle. I never planned on drinking a lot of beers that night, but I did. Before I knew what I was doing, I was out on this cold, rainy night driving my motorcycle with this old friend. I remember hitting speeds that night of over 100 miles an hour. As I watched the gravel speeding past my front tire, I noticed that sometimes the tire was barely on the asphalt of the road as I'd take the corners at high speeds.

We finally ended up in the community where we both lived. I pulled up to a stop sign and when I stopped, I fell over onto my right hand side. I was eventually able to pick my 750 Honda up into an upright position; just to have it fall down again to my left. I was utterly and completely drunk. How in the world did I just come through the wet, curving, hilly back country roads of Wisconsin? It had to have been God keeping me alive that night. I could not even keep my bike standing up at a stop sign let alone safely ride at speeds of over 100 miles an hour on wet, curving roads! Thank God for His mercy, patience and everlasting kindness! I definitely know that I kept the angels busy that night!

#18 Divine Carpet Ride

I stayed in Wisconsin awhile longer to earn some money. Wintertime was just beginning to end and the roads were clear of snow. I took my motorcycle out on the main highway and headed to work in Waukesha, Wisconsin. I was driving approximately fifty miles an hour when tragedy struck. For some reason I hadn't noticed, all of the vehicles on the highway were going real slow. It was too late before I realized why. The whole highway was covered in black ice. My motorcycle began to slip out from underneath me, my wheels slid to the right while the top of the motorcycle swayed to the left. Once again, I entered into the realm where everything began to happen in slow motion. This realm is hard to explain to people. I am not exaggerating when I say time literally seems to come to a stop.

As my motorcycle slid on its side, I began to move in rhythm with the falling bike. First I pulled my right foot up out of the way before it was smashed between the road and the bike. As it was falling over, I stepped up over the top of it. At this point, the bike was completely on its side against the asphalt still doing fifty miles an hour or so. There were crash bars on the front and back of the bike. They were designed to protect the rider and passenger but not to be used as skates on ice. Once it was sliding down the road on its side, I sat on it like it was some kind of divine carpet ride. I passed cars as I slid down the highway never veering to the left or to the right. It was like someone throwing a bowling ball down the middle of the lane for a strike. People were gaping at me as I passed them.

Eventually, the motorcycle came to a complete stop, lying on its side in the middle of the highway. When it had completely stopped, I jumped off of it and picked it back upright. I remounted my bike, put it in gear (it was still running) and went on my way. Neither my breathing nor my heart rate increased during this whole experience. I had perfect peace.

Yes, I did quit my job because my soul was of much greater value to me than the pleasures of this world. I gave them a two-week notice, packed my bags, loaded my motorcycle and headed out West. As I drove away from everyone I knew and loved, God once again took hold of my heart. I was on my way and thank God I have never looked back!

> *(Philippians 4:7) And the peace of God, which passeth all understanding, shall keep your hearts and minds through Christ Jesus.*

#19 Blood, Guts, and Flesh

I remember one time when God's mercy came upon me as I was driving a motorcycle through the mountains of Montana. I was a 21-year-old kid headed for Alaska on my motorcycle. It was early in the morning. Just a half an hour earlier I had broken camp, packed up my sleeping bag and pup tent, jumped onto my motorcycle, and was headed into Oregon on a mountain road. My plan was to take the Alcan freeway all the way up to Alaska (which at the time was nothing but a dirt road), but 1st I was going to Oregon to visit some close friends of mine.

I was driving along early in the morning praising the Lord, meditating upon the Scriptures. I was coming around a sharp corner, with banks and trees on both sides of the road. Just as I was at the sharpest point of the corner, I saw a flash of movement off to my right. Faster than I could possibly react, a large mule deer, leaped right into me. In my heart I knew instantly that it was too late. I was going to be hit by this leaping deer. At 50 miles per hour, I knew our bodies were going to be tangled together in blood, guts, skin, and hide. Mule deer flesh and human flesh was about to become as one. I saw his underside was only about two feet away from my head.

Now I am telling you that something supernatural happened at that very moment. At the very last possible second, this mule deer was lifted higher up into the air, right over the top of my head and bike. It landed on the other side of the road and continued on its way.

That is what I call the **mercy** of god! I was so overwhelmed by this act of God's **mercy** that without thinking my hands came off the steering bars of that motorcycle. I cannot tell you how long my hands were lifted up in the air praising God, but I was lost in the Holy Ghost, overwhelmed by his love and his **mercy**.

For he shall give his angels charge over thee, to keep thee in all thy ways. They shall bear thee up in their hands, lest thou dash thy foot against a stone (Psalms 91:11-12).

#20 I was Stabbed in the Face multiple times with a knife by a demon possessed women!

I drove my motorcycle to Oregon, visiting a good friend of mine, Judge Lloyd Olds and his family. While I was there I ended up working on a fishing vessel. Then I drove my motorcycle up the Alcan Freeway, caught a ferry to Alaska, and finished driving to Anchorage.

After I arrived in Anchorage, it was quickened in my heart to stop at a small full gospel church that I used to visit. It just so happened that an evangelist I had known while I was in the Navy on Adak, Alaska, was there. We spent some time reminiscing what had happened the previous year. He shared how the Lord had laid upon his heart to go to Pennsylvania to open up an outreach center in a place called Mount Union, Pennsylvania. He invited me to go to Pennsylvania with him and his wife to open this evangelistic outreach. I perceived in my heart I needed to go with them. I planned to fly back to Wisconsin where he and his wife would pick me up as they went through. However, before I left Alaska the spirit of God had one more assignment for me: a precious woman needed to be set free.

One Sunday we decided to attend a small church along the road to Fairbanks. I was the 1st to enter this little, old rustic church. When I went through the sanctuary doors I immediately noticed a strange, little elderly lady across from me sitting in the pews. She stared at me with the strangest look I have ever seen. I could sense immediately there was something demonic about her. Out of the blue this little lady jumped up, got out of the pew, and ran out of the church. I perceived that God wanted me to go minister to her.

After the service, I asked the pastor who the elderly lady was who ran out of the service. He said she was not a member of his church but she came once in a great while. He said she and her husband lived in a run-down house on a dirt road. I asked if it would be okay to go and see her. He said he had no problems with this, especially since she wasn't a part of his church. We followed the directions the pastor gave us. When we arrived at this lady's house we found it exactly as the pastor had said. It was a rundown house with its yard overflowing with old furniture and household items. I do not know how they could survive the winters in Alaska in such a poorly-built house. As we got out of the car, a little old man met us outside. It was her husband. He was thanking God as he walked toward us and said he knew we were men of God and had been sent by the Lord to help his poor tormented wife. He informed us that his wife was in their kitchen.

We went to the house having to go down the twisting cluttered garbage filled path. We entered through a screen door that led into their kitchen. When we entered the kitchen we could see his wife over at a large utility sink. Her back was to us, but we could see she was peeling carrots over her kitchen sink with a very large butcher knife. She turned to face us as I began to speak to her. I could hardly believe my eyes! This little lady's eyes were glowing red. I think a muscle rubbed my eyes at that moment thinking that maybe something got in them. But no, her eyes were glowing red. Fear tried to fill my heart as she looked at me with the big knife, a butcher's knife in her hand. Immediately I came against the spirit of fear in my heart quoting the Scripture *"God has not given me the spirit of fear, but of power love and a sound mind"*

I began to share with her about Jesus Christ. The next thing I knew she was coming right at me with her knife as if she was filled with great rage. The knife was still in her hand when she spun around. I not seen her drop it. The next thing I knew she was hitting me in the face very hard multiple times. I could feel the pressure of her hitting me on the right side of my face. As she was hitting me in the face out of my mouth came **in the Name of**

Jesus! The minute I came against this attack in the name of Jesus, she literally was picked up by an invisible power and flew across the room about 10 feet or more. She slammed against the bare wall of her kitchen and slipped down to the floor. Amazingly when she hit the wall she was not hurt. I went over to her continuing to cast the demons out of her. Once she was free she told us her terrible story. Her uncle had repeatedly molested and raped her when she was very young girl.

She thought she was free from him when he got sick and died. But then he began to visit her from the dead, continuing to molest and rape her at night. To her it was physical and real. She did not know it was a familiar spirit disguised as her uncle. This probably had gone on for over 50 years. I led her to the Lord. Sweet beautiful peace came upon her, completely changing her countenance. She was a brand-new person in Christ, finally free after almost 50 years of torment. Her and husband began to go to church with us until I left Alaska.

Years later the evangelist who was with me heard me retell this story at a church about how this woman kept slapping me. After the end of the service he came to me informing me that I was not telling this story correctly. I wondered if he thought I was exaggerating. He said that he was actually standing behind me while she was slapping me. But it wasn't her hand she was slapping me with, she had been stabbing me in the face with her knife repeatedly. He said he knew that I was a dead man because nobody could survive being stabbed in the face repeatedly with a large butcher knife. He expected to see nothing but blood, but instead saw that there was not even one Mark on my face. I did feel something hit my face but I thought it was her hand. Instead it was her knife and it could not pierce my skin! Thank God for his love and his mercy.

CHAPTER FIVE

#21 Angels Kept Scaffolding from Tumbling Down
(1977)

An evangelist and I had opened up an outreach center in Mount Union, Pennsylvania. The building was on the main street of Mount Union, being a former movie theater and theatrical facility. It was in need of much repair, having been vacant for many years. We began to refurbish it from the entrance all the way back to behind the stage curtains and screen. I think the seating capacity was close to 600; about 400 on the first floor and 200 and on the second floor balcony. There was a lot of work to be done in the main auditorium. The paint and plaster were falling off ceilings close to 40 feet high.

For us to make the repairs, we had borrowed some old scaffolding from someone who was willing to let us use it. This was back in 1978 so my recollections are not the clearest as to the height of this auditorium. It might've been higher than 40 feet. I know one thing, it was really high up and we must've had at least eight sections of scaffolding stacked on top of each other to reach to the ceiling. And, we still had to use extension poles in order to paint. Believe me, we were not using a lot of wisdom because this stack of scaffolding was extremely wobbly and unsafe. When you were on top of it, reaching towards the ceiling of the auditorium was very frightening. You had to move very, very carefully because the whole thing would sway by two or three feet, if not more. Every time that I climbed up to do plaster work or painting, I would cry out to God for his divine protection.

One day, as I was up on this scaffolding, a very notorious,

wild and excitable Pentecostal brother came in. His name was Elwood and he was a Holy Ghost-filled brother known for his wild antics. He had a car with a PA system installed with speakers on the roof in order to go around preaching. We would do what I call a hit and run evangelistic outreach in the surrounding communities. What do I mean by a hit-and-run? Usually we did this in the evening so that we would not be caught. He would stick the speakers up on top of the roof of his car; we would drive through a local community, turning the speakers up loud and preaching Jesus. Before the police would show up, we would split to another community. I'm not saying that this was using wisdom or was of God, I am simply stating that this is what we did.

So, Brother Elwood came into the auditorium shouting, "Praise the Lord, brother Mike!" I was up on the very top already trembling and moving around very carefully. The minute he came in, I knew that I was in trouble. I was not wrong. I felt him grab hold of the bottom rungs of the scaffolding and begin to climb. I yelled down at him, trying to tell him not to come up because it was not safe even for just one man. He did not hear me because he was shouting praises to the Lord, getting all worked up and excited. He kept on climbing as if this scaffolding was as solid as the mountainside. To this day I do not know why he did not recognize how it was all swaying back and forth as if it would fall over at any moment. My heart began to be filled with fear because I knew that we were about to come tumbling down. He finally got to the top, climbing in underneath the bars to where I was at. He was so excited that he began to pray and shout, crying out to God for souls; walking about on the top of this platform. This man truly loved praying, preaching, shouting and winning souls more than anything else!

I realized that there was no way that I was going to get Elwood to stop because he was going to pray, shout, dance, and whatever else as it came upon him. He was going to do what Elwood was going to do! I thought to myself, well if I'm going to die (I really believed this) I might as well die shouting with Elwood to the glory of God. So, I closed my eyes and joined in. We were praying, shouting, singing, shaking and moving about that scaffolding as if it was as solid as the Empire State building. I guess that we must've been making quite a commotion because the brother that I had come with from Alaska came into the auditorium to see what all the commotion was about. He told me later that he could hardly believe what he saw because the scaffolding was swaying so bad that he knew it was going to come down at any moment. He said that it was literally swaying back and forth, looking like it was about to tumble down at any moment. Actually, as far as it was leaning, there's no way in the natural that it could have continued to stand upright. He did not know what to do so he just stayed down below crying out to God for our protection. We must've prayed for at least 45 minutes, if not longer. I know this sounds incredible but I completely got lost in the Holy Ghost with brother Elwood.

The presence of God came upon us in a mighty way and we were having a Pentecostal, Holy Ghost, shaking and shouting service on the top of that old rickety, unstable scaffolding. I am positive that the angels of the Lord were standing all around us, keeping the scaffolding from tumbling down. Eventually we ran out of steam, sat down and just soaked in the presence of the Lord. God is so wonderful and merciful that even in our foolishness, He is there to help us!

Psalm 91:10 There shall no evil befall thee, neither shall any plague come nigh thy dwelling.11 For he shall give his angels charge over thee, to keep thee in all thy ways.12 They shall bear thee up in their hands, lest thou dash thy foot against a stone.

#22 Demonic power tried to kill me! (1977)

Here I was as a 21-year-old kid on-fire for God! I knew in my heart I was stirring things up in the satanic realm and the demonic world would try to find a way to destroy me. I did not have any fear in my heart because I had discovered the truth that "greater is He that is in me, than he that is in the world!"

Now I had a very realistic experience one night as I was sleeping. I saw this dark, faceless demon come running down the long hallway of the house I was staying in. It was just a tiny house that had actually been a chicken house converted into a small house with a guest quarters. I shared this house with an evangelist and his wife. I slept all the way down on the other side of this long narrow building. I'm not complaining (faith never grumbles or gripes). I could handle it even if it was not heated or air conditioned. The particular night, I saw in a very tangible dream this demonic spirit come running down this long hallway through the door and into my bedroom. When it came into my bedroom, it immediately jumped on top of me and began choking me. I could not physically breathe at that moment. Panic and fear overwhelmed me! Then I heard the voice of God speak to my heart, telling me to be at peace.

The Lord's presence came flooding in upon me at that very moment. I cried out to Jesus with a whisper and rebuked this demon that was choking me, in the name of Jesus. At this point I was fully awake by this time. As this dark image continued choking me, I saw a gigantic hand come down through the ceiling of my room. It grabbed this faceless, dark demonic power around the neck and ripped it off me. This gigantic hand shook it like a cat would a mouse and threw it out of the room. God's presence overwhelmed me as I was sitting up in my bed crying and weeping with joy and praising God! This experience was not just my imagination running wild, but it was literal and real!

God wants to open our eyes, guide and lead us to give us instruction through dreams. Like I said this doesn't mean every dream is of the Lord. That's why we must look at the dreams we have experienced through Christ and through the word of God. There are many examples of God giving men warnings and instructions by the use of dreams. God gave a message to King Abimelech about Abraham's wife:

But God came to Abimelech in a dream one night and said to him, "You are as good as dead because of the woman you have taken; she is a married woman." Now Abimelech had not gone near her, so he said, "Lord, will you destroy an innocent nation? Did he not say to me, 'She is my sister,' and didn't she also say, 'He is my brother'? I have done this with a clear conscience and clean hands" (Gen. 20:3-5).

#23 He Was Going to Rape & Murder My Wife! (1979)

I was working for the Broken Arrow school district as a janitor while my wife and I attended a Bible school in Oklahoma. One night at about 7:00 p.m. while I was waxing and buffing the floors in a classroom, the **unction's** of the Lord came upon me mightily. It was a divine urgency that overwhelmed my heart and my soul. Immediately I stopped what I was doing. I began to pray fervently in the spirit and also in English. I asked the Lord what was going on. He spoke to me in an almost audible voice saying, there is a man at your house right now who is there to rape and murder your wife!

*For the last couple months there had been a lot of rapes and murders going on in the Tulsa and Broken Arrow, Oklahoma area. There was literally a man hunt trying to find this man before he committed another atrocious crime. But up to this time they had been completely unsuccessful in finding him.

When I heard the voice of the Lord say this to me it shook me to the very core of my being. I did not have a phone to call her to see if she was okay. In those days there is no such thing as cell phones. And we did not have a phone in our apartment. I knew it would be too late by the time I got in my truck and drove home. I did the only thing I could I began to cry out to God for her deliverance and safety. I took authority over the demonic powers that were operating in this man. I kept praying and interceding. If you would have walked into that classroom at that moment you would've seen a man completely consumed in prayer on his knees, and in deep intercession. This continued for quite a while until all of a sudden the peace of God that passes all understanding came upon me. At that moment I knew that I knew in my heart God had divinely intervened, and that she was okay. The peace that passes all understanding had come upon my mind and my heart.

I do not get off work until after midnight, so it was rather late when I walked through the door of our apartment. When I came through the door the first thing I said to my wife was "Who came to the house tonight?" She looked at me a little surprised. She told me a man came by who said he was from children's services. I asked her what he wanted. He said they were doing a survey, and that he needed some questions to be answered. He began to ask her numerous questions about her life.

It turns out while that at that very moment he was asking my wife these personal questions, I was in deep intercessory prayer in the classroom where I was working. During that time we had another couple staying with us temporarily in our apartment. The husband's wife, Pam, came out of the back room as the stranger was talking to my wife. Now Pam is just a very small petite woman that nobody in their right mind would be at all intimidated or concerned about. This man seemed to get extremely nervous and fearful at that moment. He said he needed to get some literature from his car, and that he would be right back. He quickly left through the door of our apartment. Thank God he never did come back. My wife said they saw him driving his car away.

The next day I called the children's services to investigate what had happened. I told them precisely what had happened. They adamantly declared that they never send anyone out after five o'clock. They also said that they did not have any man working for them who go to people's homes and ask questions.

God had supernaturally and divinely intervened by placing within me a holy unction to cry out to him. Now it might be assumed that this man simply left because there is another woman in the house. Personally I do not believe this is the case. A man so possessed by devils could have easily intimidated both of the ladies, and taken advantage of them. Praise God for divine intervention and guidance.

The thief cometh not, but for to steal, and to kill, and to destroy: I am come that they might have life, and that they might have it more abundantly. I am the good shepherd: the good shepherd giveth his life for the sheep (John 10:10-11).

#24 Red Hot Skillet (1980)

In 1979 we ended up being pastors at a little church in Three Springs, Pennsylvania. The parsonage that we lived in was very old and dilapidated. There was a large porch deck over a garage area. One day my wife was walking on this deck when she broke through the flooring. Praise God, she didn't get hurt. The church did not have very much money. The amount of fuel oil we went through to keep it warm was ridiculous. I decided to put a wood stove in the parsonage. I put it in the half-basement of the house.

The floor of the basement was nothing but rocks and dirt. The wood-burning stove was a long, deep, cast-iron outfit. There was an existing chimney in the basement, so I hooked the wood stove into this chimney. It was a very old system, however, and there was so very little draft, that it was extremely hard to get a good fire going. In the process of trying to keep the fire going, I would consistently somehow place my hands against the stove. I do not know how many blisters I got from that wood stove. It seemed as if I could not help but burn my hands! You would have thought that I would have begun to believe God for wisdom not to burn my hands, but that's not what I did! Instead, I began to confess verses about the fire not being able to burn me.

This went on for a number of weeks, and sure enough, without fail, I would touch the stove by accident, and yet I was getting burned less and less. My hand or fingers would simply turn red. One day, I again touch the stove when it was literally glowing red, that's how hot the stove was. Instantly my hand hurt. I put my other hand over the burnt part of my hand and commanded the pain to cease. I confessed that I would have no blister. Sure enough, the pain left and my hand was only slightly pink.

I was cooking breakfast one morning, having just put cooking oil in a cast-iron skillet. I was making eggs, bacon, and hash browns. As I was busy making breakfast, there was a knock on the door. When I opened up the door, one of my parishioners named Paul was there. Paul and I were good friends and we would spend hours together praying and witnessing. He probably was fifteen years my senior. I invited him into the house and we began to talk about the things of God.

I had completely forgotten about the cast-iron skillet on the stove. The next thing I knew; my wife was screaming. I went into the kitchen and saw that the oil in the skillet had exploded into fire, with flames reaching as high as the old pine wood kitchen cupboards. I knew if I did not move fast the whole house would go up in flames. The house was a firetrap waiting to happen. I was not thinking. I yelled for Paul to open the outside door as I was running for the stove and the skillet. I scooped the red-hot skillet up into my hands, spun around, and carried it out the door. Paul was standing out of the way and my wife was watching everything as it happened. I ran outside and flipped the pan upside down on the ground.

After a while the flames went out. I was standing and looking down at the cast-iron skillet when I suddenly realized what I had done. I looked down at my hands in complete amazement. They should have been severely burned. All that happened was that they became a little red. Not only that, but how come the flames of the burning oil did not burn me? In just a brief period of time, all the pain and the redness in my hands were gone.

Heb 11: Who through faith subdued kingdoms, wrought righteousness, obtained promises, stopped the mouths of lions, Quenched the violence of fire, escaped the edge of the sword, out of weakness were made strong, waxed valiant in fight, turned to flight the armies of the aliens.

#25 Over the Cliff (1981)

Kathleen and I had gotten up one morning to go to Huntington, Pennsylvania. Our son, Michael, had just been born. As Kathleen was getting ready to go, I was spending time in prayer and the Word. During my quiet time, I heard the Spirit of the Lord speak to me saying that on this day the devil would try to kill us in a car accident.

(Whenever I share these experiences, I want you to know that it is not like I go around all the time saying, "God told me!" I have discovered through the years that people who are constantly saying, "God told me!" are the ones who are simply hearing their own minds speak and claiming it is God. When God speaks you will know it because what He says comes to pass!)

We got into our automobile. Kathleen was holding Michael in her arms. I told Kathleen what I had heard the Spirit of God say to me. We held hands, bound the devil and agreed that no harm would come to us or to our new baby. The only problem is that we did not bind the demonic powers from causing us to have a car accident or tell them that they could not hurt our car. It was a rainy, dismal day as we took Route 655 towards Huntington. We ended up on a back country road (one of my famous shortcuts) to go over the mountain. There is a very sharp corner on this particular road.

I was busy talking to Kathleen and driving just a little bit too fast for the wet roads when, all of a sudden, a large farmer's work truck came around this sharp curve. The truck was partly on our side of the road and there was not much of a shoulder to move over onto on this narrow, mountain road. I swerved to miss him, barely getting around him. He had almost hit us. It seemed like we were going to be okay, but just then I hit a bad dip in the road and lost complete control of the car, skidding down the road side ways. We were approaching another sharp curve where there was a small cliff to the right on my wife's side. There were no guard rails there to protect vehicles from going over the side. There definitely should have been guard rails at that turn!

At that moment, we both entered into that realm where time slows up. I vividly remember us going over that cliff sideways. The car began to roll down the cliff and I could see Michael flying through the air right above Kathleen's head. There is no way in the natural that he could have been rescued from slamming into the windshield or from bouncing around on the inside of the car like a ping-pong ball. I watched in slow motion as Kathleen reached up, put her left hand under his neck and grabbed his body with her right hand. She snatched Michael right out of the air as we were rolling down the cliff. It was supernatural!

We rolled down the cliff and ended up in a small stream. There were large rocks and boulders all around us. The car was sitting on its right side —the passenger side. Rocks pushed up against the windows. I had unbuckled myself from the seat belt and pushed my door up and away from me with all of my might to get us out of the car. After I got out, I reached in and took Michael and then helped Kathleen out of the vehicle. Amazingly, not one window of the car was broken or cracked. None of us had any wounds except for Kathleen, who had a scratch on her leg.

2 Timothy 4:18 KJV And the Lord shall deliver me from every evil work, and will preserve me unto his heavenly kingdom: to whom be glory for ever and ever. Amen.

CHAPTER SIX

#26 Gods audible voice said, "You're a Dead Man!"

I was driving into Mount Union, Pennsylvania with my wife to do some grocery shopping. I was driving a 1976 sport Ford Granada with a 302 Engine. The urge came to me to put the pedal to the metal and let it roar. The Lord had already delivered me from speeding years ago, but at that moment it was as if I allowed a devil to take over me. I willingly gave in to this urge as I mashed down the gas pedal, all the way to the metal and began to increase my speed. Yes, I knew better, but I caved and gave into temptation. My wife looked over at me just shaking her head. (Someone else was watching our newborn son Michael so he was not with us.)

I ended up accelerating to over 80 miles per hour. Kathleen was praying out loud that if we had an accident, she would not be hurt because of my stupidity and then she began to pray faster in the spirit. I was coming around the corner on Route 747 right before you enter into Mount Union when I heard the **audible voice of God** say to me, **"You are a Dead Man!"** Instantly the fear of the Lord hit me like a sledgehammer.

The voice of God and the fear of God went right to the very marrow of my bones. Instantly I knew that I was in real big trouble. I saw just ahead of me a stop signs to the left and to the right. At that very moment, I slammed on the brakes of my car, instantly slowing down. As I came almost to a complete stop a flash of white flashed past my left to the right. I mean right then and there I saw a totally white, souped-up Dodge charger come speeding through the stop sign from the left. He ran the stop sign without stopping or slowing up in the least. I mean he really had the pedal to the metal.

I'm convinced he must have been going over 80 miles an hour. If I would not have slammed on my brakes exactly when I heard the audible voice of God, his car would have slammed right into my driver's side door. There is no doubt in my mind or my heart that I would have been instantly killed. Thank God he still speaks to us today. Thank God for his long-suffering and mercy never ends.

Now you might ask: why would God have spoken to you **audibly**? I believe it was the only way he could spare my life in this situation. Notice I was not seeking for God to speak to me **audibly**, he simply did this out of his love, and mercy, even though I was completely out of his will.

#27 Our Nine Month Old Son Michael Would Have Burned to DEATH with Out an Open Vision! (1981)

While we were in Germany we bought a used Audi 100, with which we crisscrossed all over Germany, Holland, and the outskirts of France. One day as we were driving on the autobahn (German highway), I had an open vision.

All of a sudden, right in front of my eyes I saw the back seat of our car exploding in fire, with our son Michael burning alive in his car seat. This was a very disturbing image. I remember shaking my head, thinking this can't be! I tried to ignore it for a little while, but I had the vision again! I told my wife what I'd seen. She informed me that she was also seeing the same thing; that is why she had her chair leaning back, so she could grab Michael. She also had been praying in her heavenly tongues.

We pulled off to the side of the autobahn immediately, and got out of the car with Michael. I began to search high and low over the car. As Kathleen held Michael I searched underneath, in the trunk, and inside out but I could find nothing wrong. Not knowing what else to do, we all got back into the vehicle, strapped Michael back into his baby seat, and went back onto the autobahn. Kathee kept her seat back as far as possible, and put her hand on Michael.

As we were driving, the same vision burst in front of my eyes stronger than ever. The vision was so real that I could barely see what was in front of me. Now, without a shadow of doubt, I knew something was going on. That God was trying to save us from a terrible tragedy! At the same time my eyes began to water and burn from some nasty fumes. This time I pulled over to the side of the road as quickly as I could. I turned off the car and we evacuated the vehicle like it was about to explode. After I had got Kathleen and Michael far enough from the vehicle, I once again began to meticulously comb the car, which again came up with nothing wrong. The last thing to try was to pull the seat out of the back.

Since all American vehicles have their back seats attached, I wasn't sure how to do it. Yet to my surprise and delight, I discovered that the backseat was removable as I grabbed it. As I pulled it out, I was instantly overwhelmed by acidic fumes. Right underneath where Michael was sitting was a large twelve-volt battery! Acidic fumes were rolling out of its open caps at an alarming rate, bubbling and boiling. It was obvious that this battery was about to explode at any moment!

We managed to get the vehicle to a mechanic shop to be repaired. The mechanic told us that the alternator was putting out way too much amperage, perhaps due to some malfunctioning diodes. He also informed us that had we not stopped the car, the battery would definitely have exploded into flames, and our precious little boy, Michael, would have been burned to death. Many believers die early and some from tragic deaths because they are not sensitive enough to the signs from the Spirit. They are not living within what I call the Realm of Faith and obedience.

#28 The Angel's Catcher Mitt   (1983)

We were pastoring one church in Gettysburg, Pennsylvania and another one in Chambersburg, Pennsylvania. My wife was about seven months pregnant with our second son, Daniel, when the event I'm telling you about took place. (I have three sons. From the first day that we were married I always said to my wife, "Mike and his three sons.") We were out one day doing house visitation with some of our parishioners. This really sounds stupid, but it's true. My wife, my son Michael, and myself were all on a Honda 450. Of course, I was in the front of the motorcycle driving. Michael ,who was two years old, was in the middle. Close behind him was Daniel and Kathee. (Danny was still in a protective bubble called a womb).Thank God there was a sissy bar behind Kathee. We had been visiting a family from the church near Roxbury.

We were now headed home on 997, or Black Gap Road. The sun was setting, and it was glaring in my eyes. I was looking for a shortcut that I knew about. This shortcut was a dirt road. (I'm notorious for my shortcuts). As I was going along, I finally saw it to my right. It was dark, so I could not see everything. I slowed up a little bit, and then turned off onto the path. I was probably doing about forty-five miles an hour. The speed limit through this area was fifty-five, and I usually always try to stay at the upper end, endeavoring to keep the law. However, when I turned off on this shortcut, I discovered to my horror and dismay that this was not the road I was looking for. It actually was a very shallow area that was long and narrow created for semi trucks to pull over on. Now right in front of us were three major obstacles: a heavy duty steel guard rail, a large pile of big rocks, and a large wooden light pole. All of these obstacles were only about twenty feet in front of us. I knew instantly there was no way I could ever stop. Even if I would have laid the motorcycle over on its side we would still slam into all of these items at forty-five to fifty miles an hour.

It was clear that we were going to hit the rocks, guard rail, and telephone pole. I did not even have time to put on my brakes. I just cried out to Jesus. (What I'm about to tell you will sound insane, but this is what truly happened.) At that very moment, it felt like two large hands pressed against us on both sides, left and right. We were still heading for the rocks, but then we instantly stopped. It literally felt like we had either run into a big, invisible, fluffy pillow, or a very soft baseball catcher's glove. There was nothing visible in front of us to stop us. We simply ran into some invisible force.

When we had stopped, we simply fell over on our right side. We fell over onto the gravel and rocks, but we really did not fall *onto* them. I know this sounds really far-fetched and strange. But it was like we fell unto another pillow! We fell into something soft between us and the ground. Here we are laying in the dirt and gravel and an overwhelming peace was upon us. There were no skid marks in the dirt. I looked at my wife, and she looked at me. What a miracle! Little Michael wasn't even crying. Then my wife informed me that just before we got to this area she had seen two pillars of fire, one to the left of us, and one to the right.

Kathee's Interjection:

Right before the accident I remember going through a little town which had no lights, but I saw two pillars of fire, one right to our left, and one right to our right. The pillars were like brilliant, white laser lights shooting towards the heavens. I realized at that moment that they were to angels of God! I began crying and praising God while on the back of that motorcycle, thanking him for His protection and goodness.I was still praising God when I noticed that we had turned off onto a dead end alley, and we were going to crash, however, I had the peace of God. Everything happened so quickly that I knew God was indeed with us!

#29 Eating concrete at 70 mph (1984)

To do my TV programs, I had to drive all the way to Reading, Pennsylvania where there was a small, Christian cable station that had the equipment with the right price for me to do my television programs. Stan, the brother who ran this cable station, became a good friend of ours. I would do up to five 30 minute programs in one trip, that way I only had to go down there once a month, if not less. I only had one major problem. I've always had the difficulty of staying awake when the sun is shining on my face through the windshield of a car. I usually try to carry either diaper wipes or a cold, wet cloth in a bag of ice during such drives. Whenever I'd start getting tired, I'd wipe my face and sometimes I'd even have to slap my face pretty hard. On this particular day, I had not brought anything with me to fight this condition. It was a bright, summer day with the sun shining upon my face as I took the highway going towards Reading.

Unbeknownst to me, I had fallen asleep once again. My car was going down the highway doing over 60 miles an hour. How long I was asleep; I do not know. All of a sudden, the Spirit of God woke me up like somebody clapping their hands together. Instantly, I was wide awake and saw that right in front of me was a concrete wall that stretched across my path. I was just about to hit that wall going over 60 miles an hour! I had less than a second to swerve before I hit it. Whoosh! I missed it by inches. Just one second more of sleep and I would have been death by concrete. I fully believe that the Spirit of God woke me up to once again save my life.

Job 33:[14] *For God speaketh once, yea twice, yet man perceiveth it not.*[15] *In a dream, in a vision of the night, when deep sleep falleth upon men, in slumberings upon the bed;*

#30 Taking Authority Over a Dangerous Storm (1985)

One day as we were busy putting the steel sheeting on the roof of our new facility with a handful of volunteers, a violent wind storm blew in. It was coming over the top of the Allegheny Mountains, which are just two miles west from us. We could see very dark blue and purple clouds swirling violently and racing toward us. Lightning was striking everywhere in those clouds as echoes of thunder rolled across the valley. This was a fast moving thunderstorm system. If that storm was to hit us with its fierce winds, we would be in big trouble. I was on the top of the building with all of our volunteers. It seemed like all of us had stopped working at the same time. There were about fifteen of us there that day.

As I was looking at this storm, the Spirit of the Lord quickened me. Faith rose up in my heart. Every supernatural work of God is from His Spirit. I told them all to stretch forth their hands toward the storm. I pointed my hand with the rest of the men towards the storm. I declared, "In the name of **Jesus Christ** of Nazareth I rebuke this storm. I command it to split in half and go around us in the name of **Jesus Christ** right now!" Whatever God quickened to my heart is what I spoke at that moment

When I knew it was done inside of me, I turned my back to the storm and went back to work. It seemed as if this same faith also came upon the other men. As far as I know, we all turned our back to the storm and did not look back. Why? It was because we knew in our hearts that this storm had to obey. I kept on working with the men until I saw flashing and movement to my left and to my right. I stood up and looked, and this violent lightning storm was on the north and south side of us. The storm was behind us and in front of us. It had literally obeyed us. It had split right down the middle, and had gone around us. When it reached the east side of us, it joined itself back together and went on its way. We just kept on with constructing our new facility that day.

Within five months of breaking ground we had our dedication service. This first phase of construction was 15,000 square feet. The next year we added 7,500 more square feet for our Christian school. The day the steel came in for that particular edition we were still $5,000 short. Once again a man from the church drove up and handed me a check for $5,000. At the time of this book being written, we have close to 40,000 square feet of building. To God be the glory!

#31 I was a Dead Man as I Flew My Plane into the High Voltage Lines (1990)

I was in the midst of receiving my airplane license. I had finished ground school and had completed all of my cross country flying. One day I was at the York airport doing simple go-arounds (That's where you land and you just keep going after you land, and take back off again).

I later found out that the Spirit of God had quickened my wife and told her to pray for me. She had already been really upset at me for wasting all of this money on flying. The Lord told her that if she did not forgive me and get her heart right, I was going to die. She repented, and cried out to God, and said, "Lord, I give it to you. Please protect him."

Everything seemed to be going okay as I did go-arounds, but as I was getting ready to land, the wind shifted to another direction. They called me from the tower and told me that they felt it should still be okay to stay in the same pattern one more time; and that the next time around I could land in the opposite direction. As I made my approach for the runway I began to meticulously go through all of the processes of making a proper landing: I lowered my flaps, turned on my carburetor deicer, and began to bring my airspeed down to where I would be landing at about forty mph. I was still about 30 feet above the runway. Everything seemed perfectly normal.

As I began to pull back on the yoke to flare the plane, all of a sudden my speed indicator dropped to zero. As a young pilot, I did not realize what this meant. It was an indication that the wind was now coming in from behind me. This meant I had just lost all of my lift. I dropped like a rock and my plane slammed into the runway. I hit the runway very hard. I pulled back on the yoke. The minute I slammed into the runway, I bounced back up into the air like a basketball. I made a terrible mistake: instead of going around, once again I pulled back on the yoke and tried to land my plane. Once again I dropped like a rock, slamming just as hard into the runway as the last time. Not being very intelligent, I tried to land once again. This time when I bounced I was really in trouble.

Now my plane was completely turned away from the runway. There was nothing but a grassy field ahead of me with electrical power lines. I gave the little Cessna 152 full power. I kept my flaps down, in take-off position. Yet, I made another major mistake by keeping my carburetor deicer on. This means, I did not have the full horsepower of my engine. Now, I was headed right for the power lines! My airspeed was barely enough to keep me in the air. I knew that I could not turn away from the power lines. If I tried to turn away I was a dead man. Moreover, I knew that I didn't have enough skill to fly underneath them. In addition, I knew that I could not get over the top of them. If I pulled back too much on the yoke, it would cause the plane to go higher, but it would drop like a rock again, because my speed was way too slow.

At that very moment I knew I was a dead man. My whole life flashed in front of me in a matter of seconds. My heart was filled with thankfulness to God for all the wonderful things He had done for me in my life, for giving me my precious wife and four beautiful children. The second thing that hit me was tremendous sorrow and regret: I would never see my beautiful wife, Kathleen, again in this world—I would never be able to hold her in my arms, never be able to hold my three sons and precious little girl to my chest.

I desperately wanted to get on the radio and tell the tower operators to tell my wife and my children that I was so very sorry and that I loved them beyond expression. I wanted to tell my wife and kids that I wished I could be there to see them graduate from school and one day get married—to see my precious girl walking down the aisle to stand at the side of her groom. But My time had run out. I did not have time to say my good-byes. I was headed straight for the power lines.

As I approached my certain death, these electrical power lines filled my eyes. It was if the wires were magnified in size. They looked to be six inches wide in diameter. They filled the windshield of my plane.

I realize that the wires are not anywhere near that size, but as I approached them, that's how I saw them. At that moment, all I could do was cry out for Jesus. The next thing I knew, I was through the power lines. I went right through them! I did not go underneath them, and I did not go over the top of them. As I flew my plane straight ahead, I was overwhelmed with amazement, thankfulness, and tremendous joy. I kept rehearsing over and over in my mind what had just happened. Could it really be? Did I really go through the power lines? I know I did. I was headed right into the wires. Amazing! The tower kept calling out to me over the radio, "Mike, are you there? Are you okay? Please answer!"

They had, to some extent, seen what happened. When they finally got me to respond, all they could get out of me was,

"Thank You Jesus! Thank you Jesus! Thank you Jesus!" The airport radio frequency at that time was also picked up by three other airports. All the traffic controllers and radio personnel on that frequency heard me say over and over, "Thank you Jesus!"

After I landed, the mechanical personnel took the plane into the hangar. They had seen me slamming into the runway. In their thoughts, there is no way that this plane did not have structural damage. They went over it with a fine-toothed comb. Amazingly, they came back with a report that everything was absolutely fine.

> *(2 Chronicles 7:3).And when all the children of Israel saw how the Þre came down, and the glory of the LORD upon the house, they bowed themselves with their faces to the ground upon the pavement, and worshipped, and praised the LORD, saying, For he is good; for his mercy endureth for ever.*

Kathleen's perspective:

My husband had disappeared early in the morning. He probably told me where he was going while I was still asleep, but I never remembered. As the day went on, I decided to call his cell phone to Þgure out where he was. After several futile calls, I called Debra, Mike's sister, who worked in our church ofÞce at the time. Upon hearing that he had gone for flying lessons, my anger began to rise. My thoughts were, *Who does he think he is, going off and spending thousands of dollars on flying lessons, when we have enough bills to pay, and we need things for the house, the children, and me!*

Immediately, the Spirit of God arrested me and rebuked me. Within my spirit came, *which is more important, the money, or your husband's life?* Brokenness clenched my soul, and I quickly repented. Asking God to forgive me for my selfishness, I told the Lord that my husband was more important than millions of dollars, and that the money wasn't worth Mike's life!

The devil had lost the battle to keep me bitter and unforgiving and the unity between us, as husband and wife, was not broken. Directly, a spirit of fear tried to grip my heart, and I knew that fear was another tool of the devil to bring division and destruction. An urgency to pray and to stand in faith made me stop everything! To this day, I remember where I was sitting when I began to pray: right at our kitchen bar. As I sat on the bar stool reiterating my repentance of selfishness, I implored the Lord to spare Mike's life, keep him safe, and bring him back to me and the children. Little did I know that I was truly pleading for my husband's life!

Through my tears, I remember boldly declaring, "Lord, You've given Your angels charge over us, to keep us in all of our ways, even in our stupidity." My declaration continued, "In our pathway is life and there is no death. So, Father, I put Michael in your hands. I know you'll bring him home safely." At this point, I made a covenant in my heart. I made my stand, "I trust You, Lord, because there is no one else to trust. If, I can't trust You to keep Mike safe, then I can trust no one. Thank You for bringing my husband back to me!" I refused to give into bitterness, fear, or worry. My hope was in the Lord who is always faithful.

The devil had lost the fight on my side to cause division, bitterness, anger, fear, and lack of peace. I did not fail to repent and intercede for my husband when the Spirit of God dealt with me. God's grace had helped me through the test. God's faith had brought victory and brought my husband home alive. When Mike came through the door of our home that day, he told me of his near-fatal flight. My response was, "If the Lord hadn't dealt with my heart, you might have eaten those power lines!" I embraced Mike with a thankful heart and a grace in my heart towards the Lord's goodness and mercy. God surely knew what He was doing in both of our lives to keep us under His protection. If I had given into bitterness and fear, or failed to intercede and stand in faith, I may not have my husband today!

CHAPTER SEVEN

#32 Brittany's hair on fire (Christmas play)   (1994)

I have discovered through the years that when the spirit of God quickens my heart to do something, it is not the time to think, but it is time to act. I cannot tell you how many times I have immediately responded to the spirit of God to a certain situation. As I look back, I realize if I had not quickly done that which the spirit of God quickened to my heart, the end results would have been terrible and devastating. This is one of those situations.

Our youth had been practicing a wonderful Christmas Carol, in which we had a large children's choir. The men of the church had built small risers in which the youth and the children could stand upon. Starting from the front to the back, it took each child up approximately six inches. In one part of the production all the children held lit candles. Almost all the lights were turned off in the sanctuary during this time. It was a beautiful scene, with all the children having their candles lit and singing wonderful Christmas carols to the congregation.

One of our youth was a young attractive teenager who was approximately fourteen years old. Her name was Britney, who had long brown hair. She was standing approximately three rows deep on the third riser. I believe I was sitting on the front row of the chairs in a sanctuary, simply enjoying this wonderful performance of the youth. As I was watching the candlelight, singing performance I noticed something very peculiar. A very light blue haze appeared over the top of Britney's head. Immediately I knew in my heart that her hair was on fire. One of the teenagers behind her had accidentally put her candle up against Britney's hair.

Britney must have used some type of hairspray to be pre-prepared for tonight's performance, and this hairspray was extremely flammable. In my heart I knew that this could be a very devastating situation. I discovered later, that this thought was truly from God. Here is some devastating information about the tragedies resulting from hair fires.

*One of the most common characteristics of hair fires is that they are unexpected. Rarely does anyone set his or her hair on fire intentionally. Therefore, when a hair fire happens, the person is caught completely off guard and very often their instinctive reactions make it worse. The most immediate preferred reactions would be to immediately douse the head with water or to smother the fire with a towel, blanket or other suitable material. However, what typically happens is that the person will run about or drop and roll, which only fans the fire with air. Another reaction to a hair fire is to attempt to put out the fire by the use of hands, which typically results in hand and arm burns. – [Burns typical of a hair fire due to drop down]. Because burning hair will often "drop down," the person receives burns to the neck, shoulders and chest, sometimes to a greater degree than burns to the scalp. The individual's clothing may also catch on fire exacerbating these types of neck, shoulder and chest burns.

Another characteristic of a hair fire is that the person often believes they have successfully extinguished the fire and will stop their efforts to put out the fire only to find that it "re-ignites" In reality, the hair fire does not "re-ignite," but was never completely put out in the first place. If any small portion of the hair remains on fire, it will "re-ignite" the remaining hair. The final characteristic of hair fires is severe disfigurement requiring extensive plastic surgery to correct.

Of course I had no knowledge of any of this at the time, all I had was a quickening, and a super natural urgency entering my heart to get to Britney. I immediately jumped up out of my chair, running for the choir, manoeuvring pass all the other people in the play, and getting past all the props. In my supernatural rush to get to Brittany, not one time did I stumble, trip over a cord, bump into a person, or knock anything over. It is hard for me to explain to people this supernatural realm I enter in when the spirit of God takes me over.

When I finally reached the bleachers, Britney's hair was glowing bluer than ever. Somehow I got in between the children to Brittany. Of course everybody saw all my actions, and had no idea what was happening. To this day many of them that were at this performance never knew what happened. When I finally stood in front of Britney, in my heart I knew what I needed to do. I could not use my hands to put out her hair fire. Instead, somehow I grabbed the back of her head, (with her hair all burning blue now) pulling her head down to my chest. I took my suit jacket and completely enveloped her head into my chest. Miraculously, yes supernaturally I was able to get her hair extinguished in a matter of seconds.

Britney had no idea what was going on until after the service. Once the fire was out, I did not even say a word to her or anyone. I just simply helped her stand back up straight, spun around, and went back to my chair. As I think back on this particular situation, I'm sure it looked a little bit comical. The performance never stopped. The play continued, with the choir singing, holding their candle lights. In the minds of the people it was just a little burp in the performance. Thank God for the Holy Ghost, and divine intervention. I believe it was even supernatural that neither one of us received any burns whatsoever.

#33 God Asked Me: Will you die for me? (1994)

I heard the voice of God asking me: are you willing to die for me? It was as I was getting ready to leave for the Philippines. I had been to the Philippines on numerous occasions. I had been going into an area of the Philippines where the NPA was extremely active. NPA is the abbreviation for the new People's

Army, which are part of a communist movement. At that time, they were very active and they were extremely brutal and dangerous. Godly men which I have worked with in the Philippines had been murdered by them. I heard the Lord continue to say to me: if I can use your spilt blood like a seed planted into the ground to bring about a wonderful harvest, are you willing to die? When I heard the Lord say this to me, I took it very seriously. With deep sorrow in my heart and tears rolling down my face, I said yes Lord!

It was not that I was not willing to die for **Christ**, because I had been in many dangerous situations since I had been born again in 1975. I have had numerous encounters with people threatening and trying to kill me. A gang I used to run with out of Chicago tried twice. Some Yupik Indians in Alaska had tried to kill me. A demon possessed woman had stabbed me multiple times in the face and yet the knife could not penetrate my skin. A radical Muslim kept on wanting to shoot me, as he yelled and screamed in my face, with his finger ready to pull the trigger which would have sent me off into eternity, but the Holy Ghost restrained him.

Yes, I was more than willing to die, but in truth I did not want to. I had a lovely wife, 3 sons and a beautiful little girl. But I said yes Lord, if this is your will! I still remember that morning as I was getting ready to drive myself to the BWI Airport to catch a plane to the Philippines. I hugged my precious wife very tight and my four beautiful children as if it was like the last time I would ever hold them or hug them again on this side of heaven. As I looked at my little girl Stephanie she was sucking on her 2 fingers and I had lovingly nicknamed her two fingers Stephanie. My 2nd son Daniel I had nicknamed him the watermelon kid because he loved watermelon so much. I hugged my oldest son goodbye who we had nicknamed Mick which is short for Michael. my 3rd son Steven could never give enough hugs even to this day.

As I backed out of my driveway leaving my family standing on the front porch tears were rolling down my face. I said Lord you died for me, you gave everything for me, so the least I can do is to be willing to give up everything you've given me, if I can be a seed of revival for others to be born again. As I was driving towards the airport on the main highway I was weeping so hard that I could barely see where I was going. I was thanking God for the years that he had given me with my lovely wife Kathleen. I was thanking God for my 3 sons and my daughter. I was thanking God for all the opportunities he had given to me to minister the word and help others. I was also reflecting upon the fact of how many times I should been dead like many of my former buddies who were now dead. I thought back on the times before I was born again when I had overdosed, drank way too much booze, played chicken with oncoming trains, driving on the other side of the road headed right towards others. When I had been in a gunfight with a crazy man. Oh how many times God had spared me, and yet most of my worldly friends were now dead.

All of those times when God spared my life, he could've allowed me to die and go to hell. But God had rescued me, and now it was my turn to die for him, how could I say no? I remember landing in the Philippines. I was completely free from fear. In my heart of hearts, I was already a martyr for **Christ**.

Now to my wonderful amazement and my great surprise God spoke to my heart while I was over there in the communist infested area. He said: son you're not going to die! I said what Lord? He spoke to me again: you're not going to die! I remember crying with joy, I said why Lord? He said I needed to have you prove your love for me. He said I needed to have you to know that I was number 1 in your life. Even as Abraham offered up Isaac, and I gave him back, so in a sense you have offered up your wife and your children, and I give them back to you.

That has been over 23 years ago when the Lord spared my life. I'm still going to areas at times that are extremely dangerous, but I have no fear, because I know that God is with me. What if he ever asked me to offer up my life again as a seed with the shedding of my blood? All I can say is that if it ever happens again, by God's grace I'll say, yes Lord! You gave your life for me, it's the least I can do.

Be ye angry, and sin not: let not the sun go down upon your wrath: Neither give place to the devil (Ephesians 4:26-27).

#34 The Communist Were Waiting to Kill Me!

I have been in the Philippines multiple times. When I go, I work directly with a Filipino Bible college in the province of Samar. I have been told that this is one of the most poverty-stricken parts of the Philippines, and one of the most dangerous. Missionaries very rarely go there because of this. It is far away from all the modern conveniences of Manila. It is also inhabited by the New People's Army which is a Communist movement. The NPA are extremely dangerous. I have personally known Philippine pastors who I had preached with who have been killed by them.

When I was finishing up on one of my missionary journeys there, the Spirit of God quickened my heart to ask them where the most dangerous place to go to in that area was. They told me it was an island called Laoang. They said that two American missionaries had gone into Laoang, and did not come out alive. The NPA had slit their throats. As they were telling me this story, the Spirit of the Lord quickened giving me an amazing peace within my heart, telling me that I needed to go and take this place for Jesus. I told them the next time I come back, I needed to go to that island and preach the gospel. They asked me if I was serious. I said absolutely! I told them I would give them the money that they needed to make the flyers and posters to spread the word that we were coming.

About six months later, I arrived back in the Philippines with one of the men from my church who is now a pastor in the Phoenix, Arizona area. When we arrived in the province of Samar, the brethren informed us that the Communists were aware of us coming and were going to be waiting for us. I did not ask them to explain to me what they meant. I absolutely had no fear in my heart. It is hard to explain to people what it is like when you are operating in a gift of faith. It is not normal faith. It is faith that makes you know that in Christ you cannot be defeated. In the operation of this faith there is always overwhelming peace. It is the peace of God that passes all understanding. The minute you lose your peace, you need to stop and asked the Father what is wrong. This is a major way in which God leads and guides us is by his peace.

Isaiah 55:12 For ye shall go out with joy, and be led forth with peace: the mountains and the hills shall break forth before you into singing, and all the trees of the field shall clap their hands.

In order to get to this island, we were going to have to take canoes. We took the road that ran through Catarman. The main bridge was out going to Laoang, so we had to take an alternative route to get over a large river. We stayed on this road until it ran into the Philippine ocean. From there we took two large canoes. Each canoe had an outboard motor on the back of them. We would have to traverse on the ocean almost a mile to reach Laoang.

I was in the first canoe up front at the very tip of the vessel. There is great excitement and peace in my heart to see what God was about to do. I had great expectations of God manifesting himself on this island that had shut off the gospel for many years. I knew that God was going to have to perform miracles to keep us alive, and yet there was absolutely no fear within my heart, nothing but overflowing peace. As we were coming closer to the island, I could see that there were men lined up along the beach. There was no fear in my heart. There is approximately 30 men who were standing there waiting with guns and machetes in their hands.

The Filipino brothers who were navigating the canoes kept the engines of the canoes running fast enough so the canoes would drive themselves up a little bit onto the dry shore. As we approached the shore I stood up to my feet, getting ready to leave out of this canoe towards these communist. It had to be the spirit of God within me, because no sane man would lead to his death. I almost out at that moment like that picture of George Washington as he crossed the Delaware River. The minute we hit the beach, I was up and out of the canoe. The Communists were standing there waiting to kill us. The Spirit of God, the gift of faith, the peace of

God was possessing me as I began to walk towards them very rapidly. I headed right for the center of this crowd gun and machete wielding communist. As I reached them, it was like the Lord splitting the Red Sea. They separated from left to right and allowed our team of men to walk right through the midst of them.

That night we held a crusade right in the middle of the village. As our worship team was singing, the Communists and pagan religious people were marching through our meeting. We simply ignored them and kept on with the meeting. There seemed to be a very large crowd that night, probably because they wanted to see a white man. It was very seldom when Americans or Europeans came into this area. The tourists flock to Manila and Mindanao. It had been 10 years since anybody had dared come to this island to preach Christianity. The last missionaries they had murdered. Now here I was about to preach the gospel of Jesus Christ that saves, heals and delivers just like it did in the days when Jesus walked in his earthly ministry.

After the singing it was my opportunity to preach. It literally felt like the spirit of God was flowing through me like a mighty river of electricity and power. I preached under the unction of the Holy Ghost, to a great extent not thinking at all what to say, but letting the spirit have his way. When I was done preaching, there was barely enough light to make out the crowd in front of us. They had lit some torches around the meeting area, trying to bring as much light as possible. Because I could not get down into the crowd to pray for them, I had to speak the word of healing over them. I began to command their bodies to be healed in the name of Jesus Christ of Nazareth. Every time I would speak something in the name of Jesus, the interpreter would copy me in their language.

Miracles began to happen. One old lady who had been blind in one eye could now see. A little boy who had been deaf could now hear. It was too dark out for us to tell how many miracles happened that night, but to this day I have been told there is a thriving church there because of this meeting. The precious brothers we worked with had arranged for us to be put into a two-story house. We would be on the second floor, while they were going to be on the first floor. I know why they did this! They were going to make the Communists have to kill them before they would let the NPA get to us. These were the kind of men that would give their lives without hesitation for the sake of the gospel.

It was really late by the time we went to bed. They gave my friend and I some type of straw mats to lie on. We threw these mats on the wooden floor, and tried to go to sleep. During the night we could hear the Communists outside making a racket. The communist had surrounded our house with groups of men, had started little bonfires around the house where we were staying. As I went to sleep, I saw two large angels like pillars of fire in a dream with swords drawn standing over the top of the house we were in. When we woke up in the morning, it was very peaceful. And the Communists were gone.

#35 Driving A Motorcycle at Night Through Communist Infested Area under the Influence of the Holy Ghost!

We were holding meetings in a town called Pambujan, in the Philippines. God was moving in a wonderful way. The man who was over all of the work in this area is named Danny. He has two other brothers, Jonathan and Hurley, who are also ministers of the gospel. I personally knew their father, who has since gone home to be with the Lord, an amazing man of God who was instrumental in starting over five hundred churches throughout the Philippines. These men are all apostolic in nature. If I understand correctly, Danny has a sense been instrumental in starting seventy churches. Now here I was ministering with Danny. Danny came to me late at night and said he was homesick. He had never been away from his wife this long. We were pretty far from his home.

Now I had earned a reputation for being pretty good on a motorcycle. I really wasn't very good, but the Spirit of God would quicken me when I would take a motorcycle into the mountains to preach in between Crusades and conferences. I'm kind of hyperactive, so when everyone else took a siesta, I would find someone who could interpret for me and head into the mountains. We were still in a heavily populated area where there were Communists and it was extremely dangerous to be out at night. Brother Danny asked me if I would be willing to take him home in the evening. It was a rainy and foggy night. The motorcycle that was available was an old machine—I believe it was a Kawasaki 175. The headlights were very dim and the shifting mechanism could fall off if you were not careful.

When Danny asked me to take him home, the Spirit of God quickened my heart and said: take him. It was like when David had said he was thirsty for the waters of the well in Bethlehem, and three of his mighty men broke through the host of the Philistines and drew water out of the well in Bethlehem. Danny informed me that we must not stop along the way no matter what, because the Communists would be out in full force. He said we have to be very careful because the Communists would stretch piano wire across the road if they knew we were coming. He said if they got their hands on us, we would be dead men. Even with this dire warning from Daniel, I had total and perfect peace.

When we came to this town we had to take a different route than the regular road because the bridge was out. They were actually getting ready to build a brand new bridge. For some reason, when we got on the road to go to Danny's village we completely forgot this fact. We should have taken the long way around. All along this road there was construction going on.

As I was driving the motorcycle, I could barely see where I was going. I believe I was driving approximately forty-five to fifty miles an hour. I could see something dark in the pathway ahead of us. I did not know what it was, but I had total peace. I should have slowed down but I just kept on going. The next thing I knew,

Danny was yelling, "watch out." I told Danny: Hold on, we are going through it! Whatever this object was, we hit it. It turned out to be a very large pile of dirt. As we hit this hill of dirt, we were tossed up into the blackness of the sky. Pastor Danny put his head underneath my left forearm. As I was up in the air, it felt like I was just sailing through the sky. I was engulfed in black velvet. I had no fear or anxiety; peace engulfed me. It seemed like for the longest time we were not going to come down. Then we hit the road! We did not skid or slide.

The shifter fell off of the motorcycle when we hit the road. We had to stop and go back and look for it. We started from the pile of dirt and worked our way out. I did not think to measure the distance of our jump. We looked and looked. Danny was concerned about the Communists seeing the headlight of the motorcycle and hearing it running, so we decided to leave the motorbike in fifth gear and leave. As we were about four hundred feet away from the pile, I saw something gleaming on the road. We stopped and there was the shifting mechanism! We put it back on the bike, and went our way. How far we flew through the night sky, only God Knows!

#36 Over a 300' River We Go on Wet Slimy Planks in the Fog and Rain at Night, surrounded by communist!

It seemed as if we had been on the road for an hour when we came upon the river. This river was over three hundred feet wide. It was a very deep and fast moving river that flowed into the Philippine Sea. We forgot we had taken another way to get to Pambujan. The reason we had to take another way is because the bridge was out. I believe God's hand was in this. They had driven wooden pilings down into the bed of the river. It looked like they had placed rough sawn planks upon these pilings. These planks were approximately eighteen inches wide and were loosely attached on these pilings. This footbridge appeared to be four to five feet above the river. These planks were wet and slimy. I would not have wanted to walk on them in the daylight, let alone on a wet and extremely foggy night. To get to the beginning of the planks we had to go down an embankment and back up the other side. There was no way we could walk that motorcycle across this river. Danny asked, "What are we going to do?" The Spirit of God rose up in me, and I said "Hold on!" With that declaration, I throttled it!

I took off, shifting into second gear and then shifting into third gear going down the bank. Then I went up the embankment they had built to get to the planks. I came up onto the first plank. I gunned the throttle and drove the motorcycle over the wet, slimy, loose planks—not slipping one time. Over 300 feet of plank in the rain, with fog, with a very dim head light! THIS WAS GOD ALL THE WAY! If I would've gone to the left or to the right either way a half of foot, we would have plummeted into the raging river, never to be seen again. It was the Spirit of God that took us across that three-hundred-foot river in the rain and fog, over a precarious bridge that was only made for foot traffic. To make a long story short, the Lord saw us safely to Danny's house.

Years later I went on the internet to look at this river I had crossed. The internet image had been updated in 2010. The new bridge they were just beginning to build at that time has been completed. You can see the alternative road we had to take as another route until the new bridge had been built. I am overwhelmed at the amazing things I have watched God do.

CHAPTER EIGHT

#37 They were out to KILL US

We had been ministering in the province of Samar. While we were there, a minister from Manila had been attending some of our pastor conferences. In the conference, I had simply stated that we were not afraid to die for the gospel. Whether it be by the Communists or any other physical or natural disaster, nothing would stop us from doing God's will. This particular pastor seemed to be enamored with the thought that we were not afraid of the Communists. That wasn't our message. We were not there to challenge the Communists or to Americanize the Philippine nation and its people. We were there to preach the gospel of Jesus Christ.

Because we needed to contact the airline three days in advance before we were to leave, we had to have someone in Manila let them know the date we were leaving. Our tickets were open ended, meaning we could leave anytime we wanted to, we just had to let them know three days in advance. This particular minister, who seemed to be enamored with our lack of fear, was headed back to Manila. We asked him if he would please let the airlines know when we were going to be leaving. He said he would be glad to do that for us. We gave him the dates that we were leaving.

There was unrest in my soul as we said goodbye to him. There was just something about him that made me extremely hesitant to trust him. When we were finished with our meetings in Samar, we caught a plane ride back to Manila. We called this minister, and he came and picked us up in his car at the airport. When we got into his vehicle, he began to talk right away about the meetings he had lined up for us. I asked him, "What meetings are you talking about? We are to be leaving tomorrow." I asked him whether or not he had contacted the airlines for us. He informed us in a hesitant murmuring way that he had not.

The red lights began to flash in my heart right away. It's like I heard the Lord say, get on a plane tomorrow, and get out of this nation. This man has set you up to be murdered. I leaned over and told my friend what the Spirit had spoken to me. He agreed with me one hundred percent. I told him that we were sorry, but that we could not accommodate him since we were leaving the next day. He looked back at us, and basically said that's impossible. You have to give a three-day notice. You might as well go ahead and minister at the meetings I have set up. We discovered later that he had been making outrageous statements about us, making it sound like we were there to challenge the Communists and were not afraid to die. Of course, the NPA would come to kill us, not because we were preaching Jesus Christ, but because this man made it sound like we were challenging them and their movement. I did not argue with this man any longer. We stayed at his house that night.

Early in the morning, we woke up and got ready to go to the airport. We discovered he had not taken us seriously about taking us to catch a flight. We insisted that he take us immediately. Finally, he grudgingly agreed. We had him drop us off at the airport and told him he could go home. He said he would wait for us because he knew it was impossible for us to leave. We went to the main office of the airline. They informed us that our tickets could not be changed because we were flying economy and their plane had already been booked to capacity for the day. I very politely asked if there was someone higher up we could speak to. He took us to a gentleman. We explained to him we needed to leave. When he asked why, I informed him we could not give him a direct answer to his question, but we simply needed to leave. He asked us to wait a little bit for an answer. We stepped out of his office into the foyer.

After a little while, he called us back in. He told us that they were going to do it. Amazingly, they had bought us tickets from a much more expensive airline. He handed us two new tickets and told us that we better hurry to catch the flight, which was boarding at that very moment. As we ran to catch a flight, we saw the minister standing behind the rope line waiting for us. We waved goodbye to him as we headed to catch our flight home.

I know thy works: behold, I have set before thee an open door, and no man can shut it: for thou hast a little strength, and hast kept my word, and hast not denied my name (Revelation 3:8).

#39 A SAD BUT TRUE STORY!

I had a former pastor one time that lead a rebellion against me in our Christian school and our church. This gentleman had been one of the teachers in our school for a number of years (he had also been a pastor of a local church) and because of a decision I had made he had become extremely angry and upset at me. He was so upset at me that he spoke to all of our school teachers and personnel against me.

This bitterness in his heart spread like a house on fire throughout the whole ministry. Strife, gossip, and rumors about me began to spread like an incurable disease. It became so bad that after the school year, I simply had to shut the school down. I mean it was so vicious that it was impossible to keep going with our school.

James 3:16 For where envying and strife is, there is confusion and every evil work.

During this whole conflict not one time did I ever get angry, bitter or upset with him knowing that I could not afford to be bitter. The next thing that I heard was that this dear brother had been hit with a deadly and incurable disease. I began earnestly praying for him, he had been a good pastor and teacher at one time, but had allowed the seed of bitterness to spring up in him, contaminating many others with him.

One day out of the blue I received a phone call from this man's wife. She said her husband would like to speak to me. I had to press the phone tightly against my ear because he was speaking to me with barely a whisper. He asked me to please forgive him for what he had done. He said he knew he was wrong for causing all of the strife which he had caused. With tears rolling down my face I told him that he was forgiven. We spoke for a little bit longer before we both hung up. Late that same evening he passed on to be with the Lord. Praise God for his mercy and his goodness that even when we disobey him, there is still **mercy** and forgiveness available.

Hebrews 12:15 Looking diligently lest any man fail of the grace of God; lest any root of bitterness springing up trouble you, and thereby many be defiled;

We have to be careful that a root of bitterness is not allowed in any of us. It is literally a demonic seed of unbelief which rises up against the **mercy** of God that we must operate in for other people, whether they are right or wrong. We're going take a look at four stories in the Gospels how people were healed by **Jesus** because of the fact they cried out for mercy.

#40 My Wife & My Children Would Have Died. (1998)

Cutting Corners Almost Killed My Wife and My Children! We had built a homemade swimming pool at our new house. (I'm always trying to save money – which can lead to disaster.) The pool was 24 feet across and 4 feet deep. Now our house was built on the side of a small mountain. This pool was in the backyard, where right beyond it there is a very steep slope to the road below us. One day, my son Steven and my daughter Stephanie were swimming in this homemade pool. Stephanie was about 10 years old and Steven was 12. I was at my office when my wife called me on the phone. She said to me, Honey, something just doesn't look right with that swimming pool. There some water leaking out of the side. It must have been God who quickening both of us. A divine Holy Ghost **unction, urgency, a must right now** came upon me.

I told my wife, "Baby Doll Go get the kids out of the pool right now!" It is not in her nature or personality to do anything real quick, but in this instant the same Holy Ghost urgency, unction, this holy hurry up, came upon her. Thank the Lord, she did. She ran out and yelled for my son and daughter to come to her. They usually do not respond so quickly either, but his time they literally ran and swam to her. The pool up to this moment completely looked normal with no problems whatsoever. Thank God my wife was not standing at the part of the pool that is towards the steep slope. This in itself was a miracle. The kids swam, ran across the pool and came to her right away. She reached over the 4 foot wall and pulled out our daughter first and then she helped Steven get out. Now she will tell you that was a miracle in itself because of how much they weighed. It was like a supernatural strength came upon her, enabling her to lift them up, and pulled them out.

Now at that very instant, I mean at that very moment when she had both Steven and Stephanie out of the pool, the whole swimming pool completely broke loose and collapsed. The wooden walls and steel cables all came undone, swirling like a gigantic, uncontrollable snake. Over 13,500 gallons of water came flooding out; approximately 112,725 pounds of water broke loose. All of the boards, the four heavy steel cables that wrap around the pool, the pool lining and all the water broke loose. It rushed down the hill like a mighty flood onto the asphalt road over 80 feet below. It tore up the side of that hill creating great groups in the dirt and flooded the road below.

If my children would have still been in that pool, they would have been swept away, broken and tumbling in the flood of the water, steel cables, pool lining and the retaining boards. They both would have surely been killed, along with my wife, if she had been standing on the down side of the pool. Thank God for his mercy and protection! When the divine unction of God hits us, a supernatural urgency, a Holy Ghost hurry up, we need to respond immediately. If we do not respond right away, then most likely something tragic and terrible will happen.

For as many as are led by the spirit of God they are the sons of God!

Throughout the Scriptures you will see again and again when this holy unction, divine urgency came upon people. We can even see it when it comes to God sending angelic beings to rescue his people. One wonderful example is when the Lord sent the Angels to rescue Lot and his family. Lot did not want to leave behind his family members, so he began to drag his feet. I believe he was fighting against the divine unction, Holy Ghost urgency that the Lord had put in his heart. Finally, God had the Angels intervene by dragging him and his family out of the city of Sodom.

Numbers 22:23 And the ass saw the angel of the Lord standing in the way, and his sword drawn in his hand: and the ass turned aside out of the way, and went into the field: and Balaam smote the ass, to turn her into the way.

#41 The devil had me like a Fly in a Spiders Web!

Jesus said, "The Prince of this world comes, and he can find nothing in me." I'm sorry to say that this is not the experience of any Christian in this world. There are many things within our hearts, emotions and minds that are so deeply buried that we do not even realize that they are there until we are put through the flames of trials and temptation. The enemy of our soul is constantly trying to find ways to destroy us, always probing our defenses. There is a doctrine out there that declares that once one is born again, the carnal nature with its lusts and sinful desires is dead. Oh, how I wish that this were true because that would make life so easy!

However, scripture declares otherwise as well as my own personal experience in my Christian walk. Evil desires often just lie there dormant, like a seed in the soil, waiting to spring forth. The bible school that I went to taught that philosophy. I believe that the results would be shocking if one would follow up on the lives of the various graduates from this faith-based bible school. Many of them have returned to the ways of the world since they lacked a solid foundation in the entire Word of God.

Too often, Christians chase one tangent after another, failing to digest the entire Word of God. Their diets are limited and they become spiritually malnourished, never achieving maturity in the things of God. Even when I was at this world-famous faith school, the founder of this movement stood up with tears in his eyes talking about the blatant sin that was going on among the students.

Okay, back to my embarrassing story that I really do not want to share with you, but maybe it could help to rescue your life. Before I had met my wife, I had been dating my childhood sweetheart who was my next-door neighbor. I'm ashamed to say that I had a relationship with her before I knew Christ. Mentally and emotionally, she had captured my heart at a time when neither of us were born again. Actually, I discovered years later that she had not been faithful while I was in the Navy, but that is neither here nor there.

We had planned on getting married once I finished my tour in the Navy but three months before the end of my military enlistment, I had a supernatural encounter with Jesus Christ. I was gloriously born again and delivered from all of my disgustingly wicked habits and corrupt lifestyle. I enthusiastically wrote my wife to be what God had gloriously done for me. It wasn't long before I received her response: a dear John letter basically telling me to hit the road, Jack. She wanted nothing to do with my me or my relationship with Christ. That was the best thing that could have happened to me because it liberated me to go all the way for God. Unbeknownst to me, I never did fully let her go in my heart.

Over 20 years had passed with me being married to my precious wife Kathleen, the mother of our five children. We were going through a rather rough time in our lives; hence, my thoughts began to stray back to my "first love". I never spoke of my past transgressions with any glee or excitement in front of my children or my wife. I knew that could be used against them. So, if I ever shared with them what I had been through, including the fact that I had known a woman before I knew their mother, it was always with tears in my eyes. This is a major tool the devil can use against our children. Be very careful when you talk about the good old times because, as you very well know, they probably really weren't such great times after all.

Despite this, I began to wonder what ever happened to my old girlfriend. I did a little bit of investigation and discovered that she had been divorced and was now single. I should have immediately taken authority and cast down those thoughts, but our hearts are so easily led astray. I began to think about her more and more frequently. Suddenly, an idea came into my stupid, silly head which I should've known was of the devil, but I was deceived. I thought about going back to my hometown and looking her up. Of course, during this time, there was no internet that would give me access to this information. I knew in my heart that I should not be thinking like this but, hey, it was just an innocent thought. I was not planning on anything that would be wrong anyway, I just simply wanted to see how she was doing and to talk to her.

What a lie from the pit of hell! The Scriptures clearly tell us that we are extremely weak and easily led astray. This is why the minute an evil thought arises, we must immediately submit to the Lordship of Jesus Christ, resist the devil and he will flee from us. But this was not my case. I got it into my stupid head that I was going to go back to Hometown, Wisconsin and look up my old girlfriend. I went to my wife telling her that I was really missing my family back home and that I would like to take a ride out there to see some of my old friends and immediate family. She did not think for a moment that something else was going on in my heart. This is exactly how the devil sets us up. I was a little bit surprised with her response because she actually thought that it was a good idea.

Now that the idea had really taken root in my mind, I began to make plans. There was only one problem; I didn't know where she was now living and the only one who could tell me was her immediate family. At one time, her older brother was my best friend but he had completely rejected me since I had given my heart to Jesus and became a minister of the gospel.

I decided that before I went out to Wisconsin, I needed to find out where she was. I certainly didn't want to go on a wild goose chase. Believe me, at the time I had no intentions of doing anything evil, but I was like a moth that had been led to the flame. A fly caught in a spider's web. I had kept her older brother's telephone number with me through the years because they had a tool and die shop in Whitewater, Wisconsin. I finally decided to make the move, calling the telephone number to their business. Her older brother answered the phone. I spoke up that it was me, his old buddy. I carried on a conversation with him for a while, catching up on the lives of past acquaintances in the area, asking how they were all doing. I was maneuver the conversation to spring my question in a very crafty, sly and subtle way. I finally got around to it and came right out and asked him, Hey, Bro, how is your younger sister doing, naming her by name, and asking where she now lived?

His response really surprised me because out of his mouth came nothing but cuss words, telling me in no uncertain terms that what his sister was doing, where she was at, and what was happening in her life was none of my blankety-blank business. Wow, he really laid it on me, but I can truly say: **THANK GOD HE DID**!

He knew I was married, pastor-ed a church and had children. This man did not know God, and did not want to know God, but when I asked about his sister, such indignation rose up inside of him that he literally would have torn my head off if I would have been in the same room with him. Now, this may not sound like it was God, but it was God using him to rescue my poor bacon out of the fire.

After his rant, the light of heaven came flooding into my mind and my heart at that very moment I saw that the devil had set me up. There is zero doubt that if I would had gone to Wisconsin, I would have been devoured spiritually. I might have lost my precious wife, my children, my ministry and possibly even my salvation. I was like a fly in a spiders web, in which case I would have been consumed like so many others whom the devil lead astray on to the path of destruction. Thank you Lord **Jesus**, for humbling me, even by using a notorious sinner to rescue me from a spiritual guillotine.

#42 My son Daniel was dying from rabies (2000)

My son Daniel when he was 16 years old (in 2000) brought home a baby raccoon. He wanted to keep this raccoon as a pet. Immediately people began to inform me that this was illegal in the state of Pennsylvania. That in order to have a raccoon in Pennsylvania you had to purchase one from someone who was licensed by the state to sell them. The reason for this was the high rate of rabies carried among them. But stubbornness rose up in my heart against what they were telling me.

You see I had a raccoon when I was a child. Her mother had been killed on the Highway, and she had left behind a litter of her little ones. I had taken one of the little ones and bottle-fed it, naming her candy. I had a lot of fond memories of this raccoon, so when my son wanted this raccoon, against better judgment, against the law of the land, I said okay. I did not realize that baby raccoons can have the rabies virus lying dormant in them for months before it will be manifested. I knew in my heart at the time that I was wrong to let him keep this raccoon, but like so many when we are out of the will of God we justify ourselves.

We do not realize the price that we will have to pay because of our rebellion and disobedience. Daniel named his little raccoon rascal, and he was a rascal, because he was constantly getting into everything. A number of months went by, and one day my son Daniel told me he had a frightening dream. I should've known right then and there that he needed to get rid of this raccoon. He said he had a dream where rascal grew up and became big like a bear, and that it attacked him and devoured him.

Some time went by and my son Daniel began to get sick, running a high fever. One morning he came down telling me that something was majorly wrong with rascal. He said that he was wobbling all over the place, and bumping into stuff. Immediately the alarm bells went off. I asked him where his raccoon was. He informed me that rascal was in his bedroom. Immediately I went upstairs to his room, opening his bedroom door, and their rascal was acting extremely strange. He was bumping into everything, with spittle coming from his mouth. Immediately my heart was filled with great dread. I had grown up around wildlife and farm animals, and I had run into animals with rabies before.

No ifs, ands or buts, this raccoon had rabies. I immediately went to Danny asking him if the raccoon had bitten him, or if he had gotten any of rascal saliva in his wounds? He showed me his hands where he had cuts on them, informing me that he had been letting rascal lick these wounds. He had even allowed rascal to lick his mouth. Daniel did not look well, and he was running a high grade fever, and informed me that he felt dizzy. I knew in my heart we were in terrible trouble. I immediately called up the local forest ranger. They put me on the line with one of their personnel that had a lot of expertise in this area. When I informed him of what was going on, he asked me I did not know that it was illegal to take in a wild raccoon. I told him I did know, and that I had chosen to ignore the law.

He said that he would come immediately over to our house to examine this raccoon, and if necessary to take it with him. I had placed rascal in a cage, making sure I did not touch him. When the forest ranger arrived I had the cage sitting in the driveway. He examined the raccoon without touching it. You could tell that he was quite concerned about the condition of this raccoon. He looked at me with deep regret informing me that if he had ever seen an animal with rabies that according to his almost 30 years in wildlife service, this raccoon definitely had rabies. He asked me if there was anyone who had been in contact with this raccoon with any symptoms of sickness. I informed him that for the last couple days my son Daniel had not been feeling well. Matter of fact he was quite sick. When I told him the symptoms that Daniel was experiencing he was obvious shaken and upset. He told me that anybody who had been in contact with this raccoon would have to receive shots, and that from the description of what my son Daniel was going through, and for how long, that it was too late for him! He literally told me he felt from his experience that there was no hope for my son, and he would die from rabies. He loaded the raccoon up in the back of his truck, leaving me standing in my driveway weeping. He said that he would get back to me as soon as they had the test results, and that I should get ready for state officials to descend upon myself, my family and our church.

I cannot express to you at that moment the hopelessness and despair that had struck my heart. Just earlier in the spring our little girl Naomi had passed on to be with the Lord at 4 ½ years old, and now my second son Daniel was dying from rabies. Both of these situations could've been prevented if I would have simply listened to the Spirit of God! Immediately I gathered together my wife, my first son Michael, my third son Steven, and my daughter Stephanie. We all gathered around Daniels bed and began to cry out to God. We wept, cried, and prayed crying out to God. I was repenting and asking God for mercy. Daniel as he was lying on the bed running a high fever and almost delirious informed me that he was dying, and he was barely hanging on to consciousness. He knew in his heart he said that he was dying!

After everyone disbursed from his bed with great overwhelming sorrow, I went into our family room where we had a wood stove. I opened up the wood stove which still had a lot of cold ashes from the winter. Handful after handful of ashes I scooped out of the stove pouring it over my head, saturating my body, with weeping and tears of repentance and sorrow running down my face, and then I laid in the ashes. The ashes got into my eyes, mouth and nose and into my lungs, making me quite sick. I did not care, all that mattered was that God would have mercy on us, and spare my son, and all our loved ones from the rabies virus. As I lay on the floor in the ashes, crying out to God with all I had within me, you could hear the house was filled with weeping, crying and praying family members. All night long I wept and prayed, asking God to please have mercy on my stupidity. I prayed that He would remove the rabies virus not only from my son, but everyone else that had been in contact with this raccoon. I also asked God to remove the virus from the raccoon as a sign that he had heard my prayers. I continued in this state of great agony and prayer till early in the morning (about 16 hours) when suddenly the light of heaven shined upon my soul. Great peace that passes understanding overwhelmed me, I got up with victory in my heart and soul.

I went upstairs to check on my son Daniel. When I walked into his bedroom the presence of God was all over him. The fever had broken, and he was resting peacefully. Our whole house was filled with the tangible presence of God. From that minute forward he was completely healed. A couple days later I was contacted by the state informing me that to their amazement they could find nothing wrong with the raccoon. God had supernaturally removed the rabies virus not only from my son, and those in contact with rascal, but from the raccoon itself. Thank God that the Lord's mercy endures forever!

Psalm 34:19 Many are the afflictions of the righteous: but the Lord delivereth him out of them all.

#43 A falling Lamp Pole would have killed my son!

This actually happened to my son Michael a number of years ago. If you ever visit our facilities, you will see in our parking lot a number of real tall metal street lights. We installed these street lights almost 25 years ago. Now, one day Michael, my oldest son was out in the parking lot with his back to one of these heavy steel street lights. He was just standing there minding his own business looking across the parking lot, when out of the blue there was a Divine quickening in his heart to take a step over to his right side. He told me: dad I wasn't even thinking, just in my heart I knew I had to step over to the right-hand side. Now at that very moment when he moved to his right side, something came whizzing past him very close to his left shoulder and arm. Then there was a loud crash of something hitting the ground.

Here in less than a second after Michael had moved that tall, heavy and large steel street light, fell over. It slammed down right next to him on to the parking lot. If he would not have moved exactly at that moment when he did, he would' have been slammed in the head by that heavy falling steel lamp. In all probability it would have killed him instantly on the spot. Thank God for the quickening of the Holy Spirit, and Michael's quick response to that quickening. Many people die early deaths because they do not hearken to the moving of the spirit. Just a matter of inches and seconds made all the difference in the world between life and death for my son Michael. I am convinced that when we get to Heaven we will talk to many of Gods people who will tell us that they died early deaths because they did not listen or respond to this quickening. When God puts a quickening in our hearts, we need to respond immediately, without thinking.

CHAPTER NINE

#44 Radical Muslim Going to Kill Me

A Radical Muslim was going to kill my son, so I took his place!!!

I had my family with some members of the church ministering on the streets of Baltimore. We were at one of my favorite fishing holes; Lexington market. We had finished feeding the people. My wife and daughter had sung some songs. And now my son Michael was preaching a compassionate message on salvation and giving one's heart to Jesus. It was getting pretty late in the day so we were preparing to leave. About a block away from us there were some radical Muslims preaching a message of hate and racial bigotry. We always left them alone, never attacking their philosophy but simply preaching Jesus Christ is the only answer for the sin-sickened soul. As my son Michael was finishing up his message, an African-American Muslim came charging at him. He got right into my son's face screaming and yelling, cussing and swearing, getting ready to do him bodily harm.

I immediately saw what was happening and intervened. I stepped between my son and this screaming madman. I turned my face away from the Muslim, telling my son to pack up the equipment and get everybody into the van. Then I turned back to face this man who was full of the devil. My heart was filled with love for him and those who have been deceived along with him. Now that my son was out of the picture, this man's total focus was on me. He had his right hand in his pocket gripping onto something. I could see that it was in the shape of a gun pressing against the cloth of his jacket. The barrel of this gun was aimed right at my belly from all appearances.

There was absolutely no fear in my heart whatsoever as I spoke softly to him. I just kept on speaking about Jesus as he kept yelling at me. He seemed to get more infuriated that I was not intimidated. He purposely began to spit in my face as he was yelling and screaming. There were many people out on the street that day. It seemed like everything had stopped as they were watching and waiting to see what would happen. I could sense the spirit of murder and death was permeating the air. I truly believe that people were waiting for him to gun me down. There was absolutely no fear in my heart but a great sadness that I would leave behind my wife and my children. I'm sure that tears roll down my face along with his spittle as I prepared myself in my heart to die. My wife and children and those of the church had cleared away from the area. I could see them out of the corner of my eye loading into the van. My heart was filled with peace knowing they were safe.

This man would scream and yell and spit, then walk away just to come running back to me again. This continued, it seemed, for at least 15 minutes if not longer. I just was speaking to this Muslim softly about Jesus Christ when suddenly, he just simply walked away. I stood there watching him leave when an African-American lady walked up to me. She looked me straight in the eyes and said this to me. I have never in my whole life seen anything like that. You just stood there as he screamed and spit on you. We could all see there was no fear or anger in your heart. You just kept responding with kindness and gentleness.

That was my opportunity to share Jesus Christ with her, telling her that it was not me but Jesus inside of me. The Lord had spared me once again to live another day to preach the glorious gospel of Jesus Christ.

John 15:13 Greater love hath no man than this, that a man lay down his life for his friends.

#45 Saw by the Spirit He Was a Pedophile

I have a house where I rent at a very low price to single men. These men are either on assistance, getting out of jail, or even homeless. My whole purpose is to help them get back on their feet, or to help them assimilate back into society. Now to rent from me, there are certain criteria that you have to meet. My house is in a residential area so I never rent to anybody who I would consider a danger to the community. There was an older gentleman who came to me who wanted to rent a room. I **perceived** in my heart that he was a pedophile. I asked him straight out if he was on Megan's list or if he had ever committed a sexual crime! He assured me that he was not on Megan's list; neither had he ever committed a sexual crime. Once again I asked him very bluntly. He very energetically declared that no, he had never committed a sexual crime. I should have gone with that which I had **perceived** by the Spirit of God. Sometimes our natural thinking kicks in, and the enemy blinds us.

Now we also had a house that was close to our church that we would rent rooms to those who seem to be hungry for God. This older gentleman wanted to attend our church and move down to this house to be close to the church. Something in my heart was not enthusiastic about this man moving upon the church's property. In spite of the red flags, I set up an appointment for him to come and look at one of the rooms that we had available. When he arrived at our property my son Daniel was standing there with me. The minute he saw this gentleman, Dan became extremely upset. I told this man to go ahead into the house and I would be with him in a minute.

I asked my son what was wrong. He said, "Dad: I just had a vision of this man!" (This is one way that God speaks to us) I said: "Okay, tell me what you saw." He said, "Dad: this man is a pedophile!" I said, "Dan you've got to be wrong." I told him that I also had **perceived** there was something wrong with him in this area, but I told my son that I had already asked him repeatedly point-blank if he was on Megan's list, or if he had ever messed around with children. He very vocally declared that he had not. Dan told me that he had an open vision, and in this open vision, he saw this man chasing a little girl who was around six years old.

My son Daniel continued to insist that what he saw was of God, and I needed to check it out. I told him: okay, let me go talk to him. I went into the house where this man was looking at one of the rooms. I came right out and said to him, "Harvey I asked you before if you had ever committed a sexual crime, or if you were on Megan's list. You need to tell me the truth right now. I am asking you again: have you ever committed a sexual crime?" He hung his head down, and whispered: I lied, I do have a record of committing a sexual crime.

Because of my son's open vision, I asked him: who was it? With his head hung down, he said: my six-year-old niece. Now you might say, Pastor isn't there forgiveness for sexual crimes? Yes, there is! But from my experience of almost forty years of pastoring, there is such a strong demonic spirit involved in this act, that unless a person truly repents with all of their heart, and cries out to God for complete deliverance, they never get free. Yes we forgive, but we must also protect our loved ones. May God give us spiritual discernment!

#46 My Family and I Was Saved from a Terrible Death at the Mississippi River! (2007)

Many times in my life I have had vivid experiences, perceiving that God is about to do something or that something is about to take place right before it happens! Here is just one example.

On August 1, 2007 my wife, three sons, daughter and I were traveling on Highway I 35 West. We were in our Toyota crew cab pickup truck, pulling a 35 foot fifth wheel trailer. We were on vacation and headed for Yellowstone National Park. At the time, we were headed towards the downtown area of Minneapolis, Minnesota. As I was driving, I sensed in my heart that we needed to get off this highway even though our GPS was taking us the shortest route to where we were headed. I have discovered and personally experienced 20 major ways that God leads and guides. All 20 of these specific ways in which God leads and guides can be discovered in the Scriptures. What I felt is what I call a Divine unction of the Holy Ghost. It is more than a perception or a feeling. It is more like an overwhelming urgency that flows up out of your belly.

I informed my family that something definitely was wrong, that there was an urgency in my heart and we needed to get off this highway I 35 W. immediately. This is the only time that I have experienced the urgency to get off a road or highway like this. I took the nearest exit and went north towards Canada. After a while, we connected to another highway and headed west. Later in the day, we pulled into a store to take a break from driving. As we entered this facility, we noticed that there were people gathered around the TV.

We could see that some major disaster had taken place. The viewer's informed us that a bridge had collapsed over the Mississippi River earlier in the day with lots of traffic that was loaded on top of it. We could see cars, trucks, buses everywhere that had fallen into the Mississippi. Amazingly it was the highway the spirit of God Quicken my heart to get off of, it was I 35 W! If I had not left the highway, we would have been on that bridge when it collapsed into the Mississippi River. Thirteen people died that day and (145) were seriously injured. Not including all of the terrible destruction, and horrible nightmare that took place with all of those who were a part of this tragedy. Only God knows if we would've died or not if I had not been obedient to that Holy Ghost unction.

2 Timothy 4:17 Notwithstanding the Lord stood with me, and strengthened me; that by me the preaching might be fully known, and that all the Gentiles might hear: and I was delivered out of the mouth of the lion.

#47 If I Had Not Heard from God, My Family and I Would've Been Swept Away When the Dam Broke at Dell Lake in Wisconsin! (2008)

On June 8, 2008 my family and I were in Wisconsin at Dell Lake ministering in special meetings for an Indian tribe called the Ho-Chunk Nation. We were there by their invitation. They had provided the facility, and all the advertisements. We had been having some wonderful services. It was the second night of these meetings. At the end of the service out of the blue I heard the voice of God say: pack up your camper and leave tonight! It had been a long day and my flesh sure did not want to leave, but I know the voice of God. I told the sponsors of the meetings that I was sorry but I would have to go back to Pennsylvania, tonight. I could tell they were extremely disappointed. They tried to convince me to stay because God was moving in such a wonderful way, but I know the voice of God.

My family members were also disappointed. They asked me why we were leaving? They reminded me that I have never canceled or shortened my commitments. I told them I understood this. But we had to leave tonight. I did not know why. I heard the Lord tell me we must leave tonight, so tonight we will leave. We arrived back at the Dell Lake camp grounds. It was beginning to rain extremely hard. My family asked if we could simply wait until the next morning because it was late, dark and raining heavily. I said no, we must go now! I backed my truck up to the fifth wheel trailer. I saw the spirit of God come upon my 2nd son Daniel, who does not like to get wet or even really work, begin to work frantically. I mean he really began to move like in the supernatural hurry. My boys and I connected up the 5th wheel camper, we picked up all of our equipment and drew in the extended sides of the trailer.

Everybody was wet and tired as we loaded into the crew cab Toyota truck. Then, we were on our way. I noticed as I drove past the Dell Lake dam that water was rushing by like a little river on both sides of the road. Some parts of the road were already flooded. We drove through the night. There were times we had to crawl because the rain was coming down so hard, fog and strong winds. All the way through Wisconsin, Illinois and Indiana, Ohio the rain came. The wind was extremely strong. We saw 18 wheelers turned over. Lots of car accidents. Trees and debris were blowing everywhere. And yet God was protecting us.

The next day when we had finally arrived back in Pennsylvania, we discovered some shocking news. There had been hundreds of twisters and tornadoes right behind us which caused a huge amount of devastation. But that wasn't the only news. The dam at Dell Lake, Wisconsin had completely and totally collapsed. Dell Lake is the largest man-made lake in Wisconsin, and this had never happened before in all of its history. The whole lake rushed out over the town. We would have been washed away in the storm. There is video footage of this disaster on the Internet.

Psalm 124:1 If it had not been the Lord who was on our side, now may Israel say;2 If it had not been the Lord who was on our side, when men rose up against us:3 then they had swallowed us up quick, when their wrath was kindled against us:

#48 Spirit of murder on Herbert (2010)

He Was There to Murder Me & Everyone in Our Church! One day I received a phone call from a gentleman who said he desperately needed help. He was extremely mentally and emotionally tormented by devils. Immediately I perceive there was a spirit of suicide upon him. I prayed with him over the phone, encouraging him to seek the Lord, and to give his heart to Jesus. I told him that any time he needed prayer he could call me. So began a strange relationship of him calling and me praying, and taking authority over the demonic powers that were behind his problems.

Eventually this particular gentleman showed up at one of our church services. I knew in my heart that there was a heavy spirit of murder on him. I would lay my hands on him praying over him in every service, binding these tormenting and murdering evil spirits that were at work in his life. He began to come to our services on a regular basis. As I was ministering to this particular person, things began to be revealed that were extremely troubling. It turns out that he had been in a mental institution receiving extensive care, even to the point of shock treatments.

The realization of this man being capable of murdering the congregation plus others began to weigh heavily on my heart. One Sunday morning as I came across the parking lot to the church, this man was sitting in his truck just staring straight ahead. I knew immediately he had come there that morning with the intent of murder us all. It was during the time of summer, so his window was rolled down. I walked up to him, as he sat in his truck, looking him directly in the eyes. I told him: Henry (not his real name) you are not going to do it! He said! What? I told him once again: you are not going to do it, in the name of Jesus, do you hear me! He just stared at me, not saying a word. He started his truck up, pulled out of the parking lot, and went down the road.

During a time of counseling, he would tell me that he did not want to hurt his son, his daughter-in-law, or his grandchildren. I told him in the name of Jesus, binding the demonic powers, you will not do this. Now you might ask me, why did you not contact the authorities? I did contact them, informing them what was going on. Unbelievably they told me there was nothing they could do about it, until they had proof that he meant us or somebody else harm. In my investigation I also discovered that he had a permit to carry. I could hardly believe that they would give this mentally unstable man, who had been in a mental institution, given shock treatments a permit to carry!

At this point, I really sense in my heart I needed to get a permit to carry a pistol in order to protect the church members and my family. I also bought a very reliable, and good quality gun. One of the members of our church has a fire range where his son, who is a policeman, and other law officials target practice. As a young man I had been given training on shooting guns, and used to go hunting by myself at the age of 12. I had also spent time in the military, so I was not a complete stranger to firearms. I spent sufficient time shooting at this target range to where I could hit a target pretty accurately with that pistol up to 60 to 80 feet away.

I began to carry this pistol tucked beneath my belt behind my suit jacket whenever I sensed that I needed to take it to church. Sure enough, every time it was quickened in my heart to take the pistol, this gentleman would be at our church. As the months went by, I perceive that he was getting worse. One day in our Sunday morning service we had a special guest speaker who was preaching. This particular gentleman was sitting in the back of the sanctuary.

I had not told anybody about this situation but my wife and my children. Out of the blue this woman preacher stop preaching (Jack Coes daughter) and pointed her finger directly at Henry. She said out loud in front of everybody: I bind that murdering spirit in you. You will not do anyone any harm in Jesus name. People had no idea what she was talking about, but I knew. I was standing in the back of the sanctuary with my pistol tucked behind my suit coat, under my belt. After Joanna said this, she began to preach once again.

After this incident I think this gentleman only came back to our church for another month and a half, but then he just simply disappeared. That has probably been about four years ago (2010). I have no idea whatever happened to him. I still continue to pray for him, and for the safety of those he comes in to contact with. We are living in a day and age where we must be extremely sensitive to what God is telling us. Many people are dying because they do not know or are not listening to the voice of God's Holy Spirit. The Lord has rescued me and my loved ones more times than I can tell you because I heard the Lord speaking to my heart.

#49 Incredible Testimony of being Engulfed in a Consuming Fire!   (2011)

Back in 1980 I began to memorize and meditate on Scriptures declaring that fire cannot consume me.

> *Isaiah 43:2, "When thou passest through the waters, I will be with thee; and through the rivers, they shall not overflow thee: when thou walkest through the fire, thou shalt not be burned ; neither shall the flame kindle upon thee."*

I meditated on the scriptures because I kept burning myself with our woodstove. Through the years, I have maintained these scriptures in my heart. In the summer of 2011, I had an amazing experience when God used these scriptures to come to my rescue, otherwise I would have been burned to death. This particular morning, I woke up lost in the Holy Ghost. I mean, my mind and my heart was so caught up in God, I was almost drunk in the spirit. I was so heavenly minded at the time that you could even say I was not really much earthly good. In this condition I decided it was a good day to burn the large pile of brush that we had on our property.

This very large brush pile which was way over my head, and needed to be burned. It was a very, very hot day. I am sure it was over 90° outside! I took a 2-gallon plastic gas container to this pile of brush with the full intention of lighting the brush on fire. When I took the cap off this container, the container was so hot you could see the visible fumes of the gasoline in the air. I had with me one of those long stemmed lighters that you can pick up at any hardware store.

I stepped into this pile of very dry brush which was higher than my head by four or five feet. I took the gas container and began to spread gasoline over the pile by splashing it out of the container all over the brush and wood pile. The liquid gasoline was up to the edge of my feet. At the time I was not really thinking about what I was doing, I was actually meditating on the word. My son Daniel saw me put the gas container in my left hand. The fumes were visible as they were radiating out of the container. I took the lighter in my right hand and reached down to light the gas. My son Daniel saw what I was about to do and yelled at the top of his lungs, but I only heard him partly because I was so lost in the spirit. I pulled the trigger of the long stemmed lighter and instantly there was an explosion of fire and I was totally engulfed in the flames. I was completely surrounded with fire. My son Daniel said that he could not see me because the fire had swallowed me up.

I remember being in the flames of this fire and it seemed as if there was this shimmering invisible force field around me, and the heat and the flames could not penetrate this invisible force field. I remember standing being surrounded completely by fire thinking WOW, this is Awesome. And immediately at the same time something clicked in my head: you need to get out of this fire!

Immediately, I began to backtrack away from the fire walking backwards. When I was out of the fire, I looked down at my body and my clothes and not a flame had kindled upon me. The gas container in my left hand alone should have exploded, because of the fumes that were coming out of it.

Once again God had miraculously delivered me from my stupidity. My son Daniel can attest to this story for he saw the whole thing. We rejoiced in God for His great mercy! Of course, my son Daniel was extremely upset with me and was in a state of shock and amazement because he saw me engulfed in the fire. He thought surely I was a dead man!

CHAPTER TEN

#50 A Major Accident with Our Bus Prevented

It is amazing how God uses circumstances for our good. There are times that we really do not even know that God is directing our steps, but God is in the details. Here is one amazing illustration: we were getting ready to take our large 52 passengers (Van Hool) bus out to a conference in West Lafayette Indiana.

It came into my heart to check the bus out about a week before we were leaving for this conference. As far as I knew all of the mechanics of the bus, inspections and examinations were up-to-date. I simply began to check all the fluids, belts, tires and anything else that might go wrong. After I completed this task I decided to do one more walk around the bus again. As I was walking past the right middle duel wheel of the bus, I saw what looked like a small trace of oil coming from the main hub. Immediately the Spirit drew my attention to this bit of oil. Inside of my heart red lights began to go off. God used this circumstance to get my attention.

Immediately I was on the cell phone, calling up our mechanic. I told him what I was looking at, and what he thought about it? He assured me over the phone that he did not think that it was a big deal. It must have been the spirit of the Lord because I told him he needed to come over and pull this wheel. Unbeknownst to me at the time the Lord had given to me a word of knowledge that this axle had some major problems. Our mechanic agreed to come and look. About an hour later he showed up to examine the wheel. Once again he told me that he did not think it was a problem. I insisted that he Jack the bus up, and pull off the tires. This was no simple job because it was labor intense. We really did not have the equipment to do this job, especially out in the churches parking lot.

He reluctantly agreed to do it. I walked away, as he got ready to do this job.

Later in the day the mechanic walked into my office, telling me he needed to show me something. We walked over to the buss where he had removed the outer tire. He told me: Pastor if you would have drove this bus out to Indiana, you would have had a major accident. He pointed to the wheel axle, informing me that the axle bearings were totally shot. That the steel rings that kept the axle in place had been broken and stripped off completely. He said that we could have been driving down the highway, and the axle with the tires would've simply pulled right out. He informed me that he had known of other people that this had happened to, and that the accidents were always major and tragic.

We could have easily been doing 60/70 miles an hour on the turnpike, or on a back road, and lost complete control of the bus. Not only could I have been killed with all of our passengers, but possibly oncoming traffic would also have been involved. God used the circumstance of a little trace of oil by the hub of the tires in order to give me a strong premonition of danger. How many believers have lost their lives because they did not take heed to that red light within their hearts?

#51 Stop, Stop, Stop (downtown DC)   (2013)

My sons Daniel's wife to be (Catherine Yu Lee) was flying in from California in the month of February. She was coming in order to attend a woman's conference that the ladies of our church were attending in West Lafayette Indiana. We were going to have to pick her up at Dulles International Airport late in the evening. During this time, I was going through a terrible attack by the devil with terrible physical afflictions. My equilibrium was completely haywire, and everything was spinning, plus some type of flu had hit my stomach, and I was running a high fever, with chills.

Normally I would've simply driven with my wife to pick Catherine up, but I was in no physical condition to drive, or to go along with them.

It was agreed upon that my wife and my son Daniel would go pick up Catherine at the right time. As I was lying in bed, miserable as all get out, running a high fever, with chills racking my body, an urgency hit me in my heart right as they were getting ready to go. Now it would make no sense in the natural to go along with them seeing that I was so sick. When I receive a quickening of the Lord like this though I do not argue with God. My wife and son were just walking out the door to leave, when I called out from our bedroom for my wife. She came to see what I wanted, and I told her that I needed to go with them to the airport to pick up Catherine. She of course tried to encourage me to stay home, and to rest. I simply told her I needed to go with them. I wrapped myself in the back seat of my wife's Toyota Prius with a bunch of blankets, and I lay down for the journey.

It was not long before I fell asleep. It turns out that about two hours later as my wife and son were driving through DC they had become lost. They were totally, completely, and utterly lost, and confused where they were at. Now as I'm sleeping soundly in the backseat of the car, I heard the voice of God speak to me almost audibly. In bold strong words I heard the Lord say: Wake up Now! The minute I heard the Lord say this, I immediately snapped out of a deep sleep. I sat up in the back seat of the Toyota Prius completely awake and clear minded. I stuck my head between my wife and my son looking out the front window of the car. What I saw was heavy traffic all around us, and we were headed towards a signal light about 50 feet ahead of us that had just turned yellow. My wife was going too fast, and I could see that she was not going to stop.

The light turned red, but she just kept going talking to Daniel as she went along. I said to her out loud: Stop! She did not seem to hear a word I said. Again I said to her stop as she went through the red light Stop! Now heavy traffic was headed towards us from the left and from the right side. The third time I said with the voice of authority: Kathy STOP NOW! Finally, something registered in her mind, and she slammed on the brakes. Here we are stuck in the middle of the intersection with traffic headed towards us on both sides. I told her to put the car in reverse, and to back up to the signal light. Thank God she complied with me without us having a major accident. I am telling you that it was an absolute miracle that we did not get slammed by the vehicles on the left side and the right side of the car.

I could tell that a spirit of confusion had completely engulfed both of them because they were in heavy traffic, and they had gotten lost. I told her to put the car in park. Once the car was stopped at the traffic light, I jumped out of the vehicle. I opened up her car door, and told her to let me take over driving. She complied with my directions. Once the light turned green we were on our way once again, thankfully getting to the airport, and picking up Catherine.

Thank God that I had listened to the spirit of the Lord, and I had gone on this journey even though I was really sick. Thank God for the voice of the Holy Ghost that can divinely intervene even in the most precarious situations. I know that without a shadow of a doubt if I had not jumped up at the moment when I did in the backseat of the car, and encouraging my wife to stop, we would've been in a major accident! The Lord had mercy on us once again! Thank You Jesus!!!

#52 Over The Cliff, Almost in a Tour Bus! (2013)

Every time we go out to Whitehorse Christian Center God really blesses, and yet almost in every situation our faith is sorely tried. We left Whitehorse Christian center on Friday at 5 PM to come back to Gettysburg Pennsylvania. The ladies were really blessed because pastor Jeff was moving in a very profound anointing during the services. As we left everyone's hearts had been lifted to new wonderful heights. About an hour into our trip we pulled into a place to fill up the bus with diesel. The ladies all went inside while I topped off the tank. I pulled to the other side of the gasoline facility, and went inside myself to get a bite to eat. When we were done eating we all boarded the bus.

That's when things really went wild. As I was pulling out of the facility I completely lost my power steering. I stopped the bus and did a walk around to see if I could locate the problem. In the very back of the bus on the right-hand side I noticed that there was some type of oil spillage. I crawled underneath the bus to see what was wrong. From that moment forward to the end of the journey I spent many hours under that bus. It turns out that one of our power steering pumps high-pressure lines had somehow ended up against a hot engine pipe. This caused the rubber metal lined hose to melt, and for the hydraulic fluid to come spraying out.

There was no mechanics to be found, so I kept trying to repair it with what I could get my hands on. It would seem like it was fixed and then once again it would pop a leak losing all of my power steering fluid. I think we went through about 3 gallons altogether. I finally hitched a ride with a person who was at the gas station to get to and auto supply place. I picked up tape, hose clamps, a gallon of power steering fluid, a utility knife and a special tool. We went back to the bus. Once again I crawled underneath it. By this time, I would've made Elvis Presley jealous of all the grease in my hair, my jacket, and all over my body. Wow living for God is exciting!

Once again we started the bus up after I had done all the repairs, driving around the parking lot. Nope still wasn't fixed, still leaking, but not as fast. I decided to head down the road back towards Pennsylvania hoping to find a mechanic as we went, knowing that we had 14 hours of driving ahead of us. As I was driving I received a phone call from one of our parishioners who had no idea where I was at. Bob and Karen are truck drivers, and to our great delight they were about 50 miles behind us on the same highway headed back to Pennsylvania. This greatly encouraged me, and was a godsend because out of the blue Bob had called me, and was in the same area, being able to give me encouragement and some directions.

Well to make a very long story short none of the mechanics along the way could help us because the hydraulic line was a specialized hose. During this whole time the ladies were calling heaven down upon the bus, and praise God upon me giving donations to buy supplies as I kept trying to repair the hydraulic line. The ladies are to be recommended, not one of them complained, moaned or griped along that long and dangerous journey. I had no other option, if we were going to get home I was going to have to drive this forty-foot bus with no power steering. What a job, my arms are still hurting as I drove hour after hour on slippery highways, with blowing drifting snow. Praise God one of the sisters who came along had CDL license. Periodically I would stop and dump more power steering fluid into the tank, but it disappeared almost as fast as I could put it in.

In Somerset Pennsylvania I ran into a nasty snowstorm with freezing roads, but God brought us through that mess. We finally came out the side of the main tunnel underneath one of the Pennsylvania Mountains. As I came out of this tunnel a ferocious wind grabbed a hold of the bus. I mean this wind was extremely strong, pulling me off of the road towards where there should have been guard rails, but because of construction they had been removed. The whole bus was being swept right to the edge of a cliff that ended up way down in the valley below. {I mean like we were on top of a mountain, and way down below there is this Valley} I had to fight against the wind pulling the steering wheel to the left with all my might crying out to Jesus. Miraculously God rescued us right before we went over the edge. Praise the Lord we finally made it home after more than 16 hours of driving. On a normal trip it would've taken us approximately 12 hours. Thank you Jesus for another successful, exciting, and adventurous trip to Whitehorse Christian center!

#53 I Was Completely Engulfed in a Gasoline Fire! (2013)

Everything around me exploded into fire! (Tears are filling my eyes as I share this incredible story of God's protection in the midst of my stupidity.) It all began as I was stirring gasoline into a five-gallon bucket of black tar, thinning it to be spread on our Churches Steal roof! We had a thirty gallon galvanized garbage can with a LP torch under this container melting the tar! The fumes ignited and this massive wave of fire came rushing from about 20 feet away completely engulfing me. I mean I am completely swallowed up in this gasoline and black tar fire. The two buckets of gasoline are burning at my feet. The bucket of tar and gasoline I was stirring is on fire. I myself had been using an excessive amount of gas to keep my hands, arms and face free from tar. Gasoline is the only thing that would clean the black tar off me. My clothes are completely saturated in gasoline, as well as my hands, arms and face. I'm standing there in the midst of all of this fire with no fear in my heart. Just utter peace, but still knowing that I was in big trouble.

I can honestly tell you that I did not feel the heat, flames or the fire upon me. I grabbed a metal canister and put it over the top of the one bucket of gas that was burning. I quickly found another canister that I could put over the other bucket. During this time, I'm literally running in and out of the fire. I'm not thinking, I'm just moving knowing that our gymnasium and our whole church could go up in flames at any moment. We are right up against the gymnasium with a house trailer right there. The apartment and the stairs to the apartment above our gymnasium were right there. I had to get the fire out, and I mean fast! Everything was on fire including the ground where we had spilled tar and gas.

The whole place is nothing but an infernal. During this time, Jesse had made his way around the flames nurturing his burnt arm, which he had received standing outside of the flames! He was trying to find a water hose we had laying there to water a small garden. I'm still running in and out of the flames trying to put out this raging fire. Jesse had been through a terrible fire in the past, being seriously hurt. I could see that he was in the midst of some shock from the fire and the heat.

Right before my very eyes, the bucket that was filled with tar and gasoline had melted at my feet to less than 8 inches high. Now the flames were getting worse, they were reaching high into the sky. The men who have been spreading the mixture of tar and Gasoline come running seeing the flames on top of our Church Sanctuary. The whole thing was nothing but a massive blaze. During this time, brother Mark, who lives in the apartment up above, comes running out onto the deck of his apartment. He sees everything that is happening.

Brother Jesse is wrestling with the water hose, trying to disconnect it from another hose in order that we can use it to fight the fire. I ran over and began to help him. And then I took the hoses from him, heading back into the fire. Praise God the water did the job even with gasoline and burning tar everywhere. We were able to douse the flames. Praise God, praise God, praise God the fire was out.

Things happened so fast at the time that I did not even realize exactly the events that had transpired. But God in His grace and in His mercy once again protected me from my own massive stupidity. Jesse did receive burns on his right forearm. Amazingly, I did not receive one burn, not one singed hair or even the smell of smoke on me. All of the gas that was on me, my hands, my face and my clothes never ignited. God is so good! His Mercy Endures Forever!

#54 Angelic Protection From A Logging Truck. (2013)

My wife and I went to her mother's house too install a small satellite dish system, with the receiver. Her mother was filled with great anticipation to watch our network on the small dish (WBNTV). After we had installed the system, we ate lunch, and headed back home to Gettysburg Pennsylvania. We took route 994 from Cassville, through three Springs, to Orbisonia, PA. When we entered Orbisonia, we turned right onto Route 522 towards McConnellsburg, Pennsylvania. My wife and I were having a wonderful time just sharing and talking about the goodness of God, while at the same time obeying the speed limit. As we were coming around a rather sharp turn, I saw on the other side of the road a logging truck just coming around this curve, and coming way to fast.

This logging truck definitely was coming around that corner way faster than what it should have been. Not only was this 18 Wheeler Going Way to fast, but it was fully loaded with logs to the very top of its steel racks. At that very moment out of the corner of my left eye I seem to see something flying loose at the very end of the truck. This truck was going so fast that as it roared past us the wind of its passage literally began to push our little Toyota Prius right off of the road. Then suddenly out of the blue, I saw something heading for our windshield, and towards the front of the car. My wife also saw this object coming towards us, automatically threw her hands and arms up in front of her face to try to protect herself. Right before this object hit us though there was a gigantic burst of a bright white light. This fluffy white cloud got between us and the oncoming object.

At that very moment something struck our windshield and our vehicle so hard, that Our vehicle shook so violently that it felt like we were going to be flipped end over end. This all happened extremely fast because we were doing approximately 55 miles an hour, with the logging truck going past us going in the opposite direction faster than the speed limit. My wife at that moment per her hands over her ears because we heard a horrendous crashing sound hitting our little Prius. Now as fast as it happened it was over. My wife yelled as the logging truck continued on its way, never slowing down even for one moment: "what was that!"

Oh I can tell you that we are so blessed to be alive! We couldn't believe that the windshield was still whole in front of us, with not even one crack or chip! I immediately pulled the vehicle off to the edge of the road and stopped in order to take a look at the damage. Surely whatever had hit us must have taken out the whole front part of the car, including its left side. I got out of the vehicle, and exam that car very carefully from top to bottom. Amazingly we found not even one scratch or dent on the Prius! As I got back into the vehicle, and drove down the road my wife and I both declared that we had just beheld a wonderful and marvelous angelic miracle.

We are now convinced that an angel got between us and a loose flying logging chain from the logging truck. We both saw a flash of white light that enveloped the whole front of the vehicle a split second before we were hit, and the car shook with a loud crashing sound. This logging chain, without God's divine intervention, would have cut through our car like a guillotine, or a red-hot knife on a stick of soft butter. It would have taken off the top of our car, cutting both my wife and I into half. What an amazing and wonderful God that we serve. Once again he had sent his angelic beings to protect us. We are so thankful for the goodness of God and His angelic protection!

How to Live in the Miraculous!

This is a quick explanation of how to live and move in the realm of the miraculous. Seeing divine interventions of God is not something that just spontaneously happens because you have been born-again. There are certain biblical principles and truths that must be evident in your life. This is a very basic list of some of these truths and laws:

1.   You must give Jesus Christ your whole heart. You cannot be lackadaisical in this endeavour. Being lukewarm in your walk with God is repulsive to the Lord. He wants 100% commitment. Jesus gave His all, now it is our turn to give our all. He loved us 100%. Now we must love Him 100%.

My son, give me thine heart, and let thine eyes observe my ways (Proverbs 23:26).

So then because thou art lukewarm, and neither cold nor hot, I will spew thee out of my mouth (Revelation 3:16).

2. There must be a complete agreement with God's Word. We must be in harmony with the Lord in our attitude, actions, thoughts, and deeds. Whatever the Word of God declares in the New Testament is what we wholeheartedly agree with.

Can two walk together, except they be agreed? (Amos 3:3).

For the eyes of the LORD run to and fro throughout the whole earth, to shew himself strong in the behalf of them whose heart is perfect toward him (2 Chronicles 16:9).

3. Obey and do the Word from the heart, from the simplest to the most complicated request or command. No matter what the Word says to do, do it! Here are some simple examples: Lift your hands in praise, in everything give thanks, forgive instantly, gather together with the saints, and give offerings to the Lord, and so on.

> *I can of mine own self do nothing: as I hear, I judge: and my judgment is just; because I seek not mine own will, but the will of the Father which hath sent me (John 5:30).*

4. Make Jesus the highest priority of your life. Everything you do, do not do it as unto men, but do it as unto God.

> *If ye then be risen with Christ, seek those things which are above, where Christ sitteth on the right hand of God. Set your affection on things above, not on things on the earth (Colossians 3:1-2).*

5. Die to self! The old man says, "My will be done!" The new man says, "God's will be done!"

> *I am crucified with Christ: nevertheless I live; yet not I, but Christ liveth in me: and the life which I now live in the flesh I live by the faith of the Son of God, who loved me, and gave himself for me (Galatians 2:20).*

> *Now if we be dead with Christ, we believe that we shall also live with him (Romans 6:8).*

6. Repent the minute you get out of God's will—no matter how minor, or small the sin may seem.

> *(Revelation 3:19).*

> *As many as I love, I rebuke and chasten: be zealous therefore, and repent.*

7. Take one step at a time. God will test you (not to do evil) to see

if you will obey him. *Whatever He tells you to do: by His Word, by His Spirit, or within your conscience, do it.* He will never tell you to do something contrary to His nature or His Word!

> **For whosoever shall do the will of my Father which is in heaven, the same is my brother, and sister, and mother (Matthew 12:50).**

> **Then went he down, and dipped himself seven times in Jordan, according to the saying of the man of God: and his flesh came again like unto the flesh of a little child, and he was clean (2 Kings 5:14).**

ABOUT THE AUTHOR

Dr. Michael and Kathleen Yeager have served as pastors/apostles, missionaries, evangelists, broadcasters and authors for over four decades. They flow in the gifts of the Holy Spirit, teaching the Word of God with wonderful signs and miracles following in confirmation of God's Word. In 1983, they began Jesus is Lord Ministries International, where are the pastors to this date.

Websites Connected to Doc Yeager

www.docyeager.com

www.jilmi.org

www.wbntv.org

<u>Books Written by Doc Yeager:</u>

"Living in the Realm of the Miraculous #1"
"I need God Cause I'm Stupid"
"The Miracles of Smith Wigglesworth"
"How Faith Comes 28 WAYS"
"Horrors of Hell, Splendors of Heaven"
"The Coming Great Awakening"
"Sinners in The Hands of an Angry GOD", (modernized)
"Brain Parasite Epidemic"
"My JOURNEY to HELL" - illustrated for teenagers
"Divine Revelation of Jesus Christ"
"My Daily Meditations"
"Holy Bible of JESUS CHRIST"
"War In The Heavenlies - (Chronicles of Micah)"
"Living in the Realm of the Miraculous #2"
"My Legal Rights to Witness"
"Why We (MUST) Gather! - 30 Biblical Reasons"
"My Incredible, Supernatural, Divine Experiences"
"Living in the Realm of the Miraculous #3"
"How GOD Leads & Guides! - 20 Ways"
"Weapons of Our Warfare"
"How You Can Be Healed"
"God Still Heals"
"God Still Provides"
"God Still Protects"

Made in the USA
Las Vegas, NV
02 December 2022